I HAVE CANCER, AND I DON'T KNOW WHAT TO DO.

A PRACTICAL STEP BY STEP GUIDE TO NAVIGATING YOUR CANCER JOURNEY

ROMEO RICHARDS

Upcoming Books

Book One
Rethinking Healthcare

Book Two
Children Need Love, Not Drugs

Book Three
Access To A Waiting List is Not Access To Healthcare

Book Four
Why Medical Schools Need Reform

This book is a comprehensive guide to navigating the journey from the moment you receive a cancer diagnosis. Designed to save you countless hours of questioning and searching through the internet and local libraries, it consolidates essential information from hundreds of reliable sources into one accessible handbook. Unlike many online sources that are often untrustworthy and commercially motivated, our goal is not to sell you anything. We aim to alleviate your distress and confusion by providing trustworthy, essential information to help you during this challenging time.

If you're too unwell to read the entire book, focus on the 'Action Steps' in each section. These will give you sufficient information to begin.

Disclaimer:

This book is designed to serve as an educational and informational resource. It is not intended to replace professional medical advice or to be used for diagnosing health conditions. For personalised guidance and treatment options, it is crucial to consult with a qualified medical doctor who can provide recommendations tailored to your specific medical situation.

I Have Cancer, and
I Don't Know What To Do

Romeo Richards

Published by
The Business Education Center
info@romeorichards.uk

ISBN: 978-1-915806-02-4

Dedication

This book is dedicated to the memory of my brother, Siekie, and my friends, Besman and Rob. Your passing will inspire changes in healthcare, ultimately saving and improving the lives of others.

"Cancer can take away all of my physical abilities. It cannot touch my mind, it cannot touch my heart, and it cannot touch my soul."

- Jim Valvano,
basketball player,
coach, and broadcaster

Table of Contents

Why You Should Read This Book

When my friend Besman was diagnosed with lung cancer, we were shell-shocked. We have all heard about cancer. However, the typical human attitude is that would never happen to us until we hear the three dreaded words: "You have cancer".

More than being shocked, we felt powerless. We knew nothing about cancer. Unless you have a particular interest in the subject or are a medical professional, not many people spend their time researching cancer. Until, of course, you or a loved one is diagnosed with it.

Most people who receive that news scramble for information. However, with so many sources of information, that can feel overwhelming. Most people freeze because they do not know where to start. It's as if they are pulled in different directions simultaneously.

The oncologist who has been treating cancer patients for decades breaks the news to you the novice patient, and asks you, who knows nothing about cancer, to make treatment decisions. How can someone with no prior knowledge of cancer, having just received the dreadful news, be expected to make sound decisions?

Then there are the vultures who prey on your ignorance and anxiety to sell you their snake oil. They know you are desperate, so they choose your moment of vulnerability to extort your money.

This book guides you through the fog of cancer diagnosis and treatment, so you don't feel like a deer in the headlights.

As we delve into the subject, the book guides you through a comprehensive exploration of your cancer journey, from your initial diagnosis and medical interventions to non-medical and practical support. It provides a holistic understanding of cancer, not merely as a medical condition but as a profound human experience, by drawing on a blend of rigorous research, expert insights, and deeply personal narratives.

The first thing I would like you to know is that cancer is no longer a death sentence. So stay calm. You can be cured. No, you will be cured. Simply follow the steps in this book for a better outcome.

This book is a cancer crash course that aims to limit your anxiety and point you in the right direction. With all its complexities, cancer challenges us to look beyond the confines of biology and medicine. It invites us to explore the human spirit, resilience, and the profound interconnectedness of our physical, emotional, and psychological realms. Through this book, we will embark on an intricate journey of understanding, hope, and solace.

Facing a cancer diagnosis is undeniably challenging. However, understanding what it entails is the first step towards recovery. With informed decisions, support, and consistent education, you can chart a path marked by hope, resilience, and informed choices.

I promised my friend Besman that I would tell his story. Most importantly, I would use my pain to help others in similar situations. I hope this book guides you in your journey to recovery. As bad as things might appear now, know that you will not only survive cancer; you will prevail and grow.

Introduction

"You have cancer". Those three dreaded words can have a devastating impact on anyone's life. People usually experience shock, fear, disbelief, and anxiety. In addition to the emotional reaction, most are typically clueless about what follows. A cancer diagnosis can turn your world upside-down. You immediately set aside all your plans and projects as you embark on your path to recovery. In addition to being forced to make complex treatment decisions, you must also make practical day-to-day survival decisions. That can prove overwhelming, which is where this cancer recovery handbook comes in.

It provides information that blends medical treatments with holistic therapies, dietary changes, and physical activities to enable you to harness a comprehensive recovery approach. The road to cancer recovery is paved with ups and downs, defeats and victories, good days and sleepless nights. Increasing the number of good days and decreasing the sleepless nights requires an effective plan.

This handbook aims to provide you with such a plan. It offers you strategies for the following:

- dealing with the initial diagnosis,
- clarifying questions to ask your healthcare providers,
- understanding the nuances of your diagnosis,

- seeking emotional support,
- choosing the best treatment options,
- coping with treatment side-effects,
- seeking a second opinion,
- choosing non-medical interventions,
- incorporating lifestyle changes,
- enrolling in clinical trials,
- dealing with financial and other day-to-day activities,
- finding useful resources.

Cancer is undeniably challenging. Yet, amid the emotions and pressing medical demands, please remember you are not alone. By seeking clarity about the type and stage of your cancer, leaning on your support network, and taking proactive steps, you can navigate your path to recovery with resilience and hope. The recovery journey is doubtless long and tedious. However, with preparation and understanding, it's one that you can traverse with strength and determination. Please carry this handbook as your guide along the way.

Chapter One: Be Hopeful: Cancer is No Longer a Death Sentence

The words "You have cancer" are probably the three most dreaded words, topped only by the 1980s' "You have AIDS". Those were the days when your doctor said you had AIDS, it was inevitably game over for you.

These days, science has advanced to the point where no one dies from AIDS. The disease has almost disappeared. Well, a similar thing is happening in cancer country. Granted, about a thousand people still die from cancer each day. However, that number is minuscule compared to the number of people diagnosed with the disease. Cancer, once a word that meant finality, has become a journey of resilience. Due to advances in medical science, the landscape of cancer treatment and the survival rate have been transformed, giving rise to a new era of recovery and hope.

The current rate of cancer deaths is 146.2 per 100,000.[1] Yes, every single death is one too many. However, there is more reason to be hopeful than ever. Even though cancer survival rates depend upon factors such as cancer type, stage at diagnosis, and patient demographics such as age and race, statistics on survival rates are a ray of hope in a very challenging terrain.

The overall cancer survival rate has increased from 49% in the 1970s to 70% for Caucasians[2] and 39% to 63% for those of African heritage. Surviving for five years is the metric commonly used to measure cancer survival. The percentage of patients still alive at least five years after their initial cancer diagnosis shows progress. That figure continues to improve for most cancer types. For example, the five-year survival rate for prostate cancer has reached almost 100%.[3]

> The breast cancer five-year survival rate currently stands at approximately 90% in most OECD countries.[4] Similarly, childhood leukaemia, once a grim diagnosis, now boasts survival rates exceeding 85%. Colorectal cancer survivability is around 65%.[5] While still deadly, the survival rate of lung cancer patients is slowly but steadily increasing. These outcomes result from early detection, screening, minimally invasive surgical techniques, and ground-breaking targeted therapies.

It would be dishonest to suggest that anything to do with cancer is easy. The brutality of the treatment alone is enough to send shock waves through the bravest person. Despite that, you must have hope. Decades ago, when people heard the words *you have cancer*, they knew it was game over. As brutal as the treatment is today, the majority of people survive cancer. Therefore, you will survive. The possibility of you being one of the handful of people who die from cancer is very low.

I know I said the death of a friend from cancer inspired this handbook. Therefore, it might sound ironic that I ask you to be hopeful. My friend died due to a late diagnosis and lack of information. If we had been privy to the information in this handbook at the time, the outcome might have been very different despite his late diagnosis. That is my motivation for making this information available to you. I want to ensure that you do not suffer my friend's fate.

During the final days of my friend's life, we were desperately searching for CBD to relieve his pain, but we could not find any. At one point, we contemplated flying to The Netherlands to get it. Only a handful of general practitioners were legally allowed to prescribe it then. These days, CBD is everywhere. Additionally, we sought a second opinion but did not know how to go about it. We wanted to get him into a clinical trial, but again, we had no idea how to proceed.

You will find all the information we lacked and more in this handbook. So, when I say you need to be hopeful, you must be because if we had been in possession of this manual, my friend might still be alive.

No doubt, the path from diagnosis to survivorship is laced with unnerving challenges. However, the advances in effective treatments and consistently improving survival rates should inspire you. The key is to approach treatment proactively and maintain a positive outlook.

Your state of mind is a powerful determinant of the outcome of your treatment journey. Cultivating hope and maintaining a positive outlook provide emotional benefits and physiologically impact your treatment outcome.

Hope does the following:

- **Improves Immune Response**: A positive psychological response to cancer treatment improves and strengthens your immune system,

- **Helps a Speedy Physical Recovery**: Positive emotions lead to faster healing from wounds and surgical procedures,
- **Lowers the Perception of Pain**: Hope and positivity can control pain perception, reducing discomfort and increasing tolerance.

Hope and a positive outlook are essential therapeutic elements in the healing process. They empower you to face your diagnosis with courage and actively participate in your treatment and recovery. You can improve your quality of life and clinical outcomes by nurturing these psychological resources.

Hope and a positive outlook are essential parts of the healing process. They are not just feel-good platitudes; they have a tangible impact on the physiological aspects of healing. A hopeful attitude encourages adherence to treatment directives, proactive engagement in recovery, and improved immune function.

Hope and a positive outlook are essential parts of the healing process. They are not just feel-good platitudes; they have a tangible impact on the physiological aspects of healing.

When you maintain a positive outlook, you experience less distress and better manage the side effects of your treatment. Hope is a critical factor in controlling the uncertainty and anxiety brought about by a cancer diagnosis. It is only hope that fuels the requisite perseverance to endure the treatment.

The Emotional Response to a Cancer Diagnosis

According to a report by the American Cancer Society most newly diagnosed patients report feelings of shock and disbelief.[6] In a bid to protect itself, the human mind may enter a denial phase as a coping mechanism against the overwhelming news.

As the initial shock subsides, a plethora of other emotions emerge. Feelings of fear and anxiety, often related to concerns about the future, treatment, and implications for loved ones, become prevalent. Simultaneously, feelings of sadness and grief over the anticipated changes and losses, anger, and sometimes even guilt, often stemming from thoughts of potential causes, can engulf the person concerned.

- **Fear and Anxiety**: The disease's unknown trajectory, concerns about treatment, side effects, and potential outcomes often culminate in anxiety. The fear of physical pain, changes in appearance, and death also loom large.[7]
- **Anger**: The "why me?" sentiment can lead to resentment and anger. Anger stems from a perceived loss of control over one's life and body.[8]
- **Sadness and Grief**: Mourning the loss of the 'pre-cancer' self, grieving potential future losses, and processing the entire situation can often lead to profound sadness.[9]
- **Guilt**: Many wonder if they could've done something different to prevent the disease, leading to unnecessary and unhelpful self-blame.

Understanding that these feelings are natural and almost universal among cancer patients is the first step towards emotional healing.

Techniques for Effectively Managing Stress and Anxiety

Actively engaging in stress-relieving activities can serve as a buffer against the emotional tumult brought on by a cancer diagnosis.

Mindfulness and Meditation: Techniques such as guided imagery, progressive muscle relaxation, and mindfulness meditation reduce anxiety and enhance mood in cancer patients.[10]

Deep Breathing: Simple deep breathing exercises calm the nervous system, reducing feelings of panic and anxiety.[11]

Physical Activity: Regular, moderate exercise boosts mood by releasing endorphins, the body's natural stress-relievers.[12]

Journaling: Writing about one's feelings can offer clarity and be an emotional outlet.[13]

Music and Art Therapy: Engaging in creative outlets can provide a distraction and act as a medium for expression.[14]

The emotional and psychological realms of the cancer journey, while challenging, are integral to holistic healing. By acknowledging feelings, seeking support, and actively managing stress, you can cultivate resilience and navigate your path with strength and hope.

Strategies for Cultivating and Maintaining a Hopeful Environment

Hope is a crucial source of strength for traversing the cancer journey. However, hope does not appear in a vacuum. You must purposefully create a hopeful environment. Cultivating optimism when you have cancer is challenging but necessary.

Strategies for cultivating a hopeful environment include the following:

Set mini goals: You must set short-term, realistic, achievable goals. Developing a habit of small wins creates momentum and provides direction and a sense of control over your future.

Maintain Normalcy: I understand it is easier said than done. Maintaining normalcy in the face of a cancer diagnosis can be challenging. However, that's precisely what you must do to maintain sanity. Continue your daily routines, attend work if you have the strength, and maintain your family chores as much as possible.

Seek information: Educate yourself about cancer. Find out everything you can about your condition and treatment options. Information is empowering and alleviates fears of the unknown.

Nurture your connections: Build a strong support network to provide emotional support. Engaging with family and friends during difficult times is critical to your healing process. Your friends and family provide the emotional sustenance you need for your cancer journey.

Join support groups: Being a part of a community is also essential for healing. Connecting with others going through similar experiences reduces feelings of isolation. It provides an opportunity for trading stories and coping strategies.

Find meaning: Engage in activities that offer a sense of purpose. A meaningful activity does not necessarily have to be work. A hobby that provides fulfilment through volunteering or engaging in creative self-expression such as art, writing, painting, or music provides distraction, a sense of normalcy, and a source of accomplishment.

Engage in spirituality: If you have a spiritual or religious belief, this is the best time to embrace it wholeheartedly. Engaging in spiritual or religious practices offers a sense of meaning, comfort, and hope in times of crisis.

Practice mindfulness: Engage in mindfulness or meditation. Quieting the mind reduces stress and promotes relaxation and a positive state of mind. Try to rid your mind of negative thoughts as much as possible. Visualise the outcomes you seek for your treatment. Positive visualisations reinforce a sense of hope.

Proactive engagement in treatment: Become actively engaged in your treatment. Discuss all treatment options, including clinical trials and second opinions. Active engagement in your treatment provides a sense of control, and control leads to hope.

Make lifestyle changes: Eat a healthy diet. Nutrition provides the fuel the body needs for recovery. Also, engage in physical activities. Physical activity does not necessarily mean sport. You might not have the strength for sporting activity.

The goal is simply to move. And finally, sleep. Recovery takes place while you are asleep. So, get as much sleep as possible.

Seek external inspiration: Reading or listening to inspirational stories of those who, against the odds, survived cancer can be a source of hope. At the same time, stay away from negative stories. A cancer diagnosis is harmful enough. You do not want additional negativity.

Be grateful: Celebrate small wins. Gratitude is the glue that holds everything together. Cancer is not about big wins; they seldom come. It's about celebrating every victory along the way, even if it's getting out of bed or swallowing a couple of spoons of your meal. You need to be grateful for every little daily victory.

ACTION PLAN

Hope and positivity are essential for fighting cancer. As difficult as it is to be hopeful when facing a formidable enemy such as cancer, hope makes all the difference to your outcome. Hope is beneficial not only for psychological resilience but also for physiological impact.

Take the following action steps:

Step One

In medicine, accurate diagnosis is fifty per cent of the cure. So, ensure you learn everything there is to know about your specific type of cancer.

Ask your healthcare providers as many questions as possible about your prognosis and treatment options, and conduct your own research using credible sources.

Step Two

Cancer is brutal; you cannot fight it on your own. So, enlist the emotional support of your friends, family, and support groups. Seek the help of mental health professionals such as counsellors or therapists. Draw strength from stories of cancer survivors.

Step Three

Cancer treatment is constantly evolving. As mentioned above, cancer is no longer a death sentence. So, seek information on the latest research and advancements in cancer treatment. Ask your healthcare providers about the latest studies or clinical trials relevant to your care.

Step Four

You get what you focus on. Yes, you might be in bad shape now, but look toward to the future. Set future goals and milestones to achieve after your treatment. Focusing on the future helps make the present bearable.

Hope is a good thing, and good things never die.

Hope is a good thing, and good things never die.

Chapter Two: Clarifying Questions to Ask Your Doctor

A cancer diagnosis is often followed by the question: "Why me?" Afterwards, come questions such as: "What does this diagnosis mean?" "How will this affect my loved ones?" and perhaps the most crucial question of all, "What comes next?". To answer these questions, you first need to ask your healthcare providers some clarifying questions to enable you plot your path forward. It isn't easy to adequately plan a smooth path without answers to those clarifying questions.

The key to minimising the anguish of a cancer diagnosis is open and proactive engagement and communication with your doctor and other healthcare providers to gather essential information and make informed decisions.

As we pointed out in Chapter One, a cancer diagnosis can be overwhelming. Therefore, ensure you are accompanied by someone when attending your appointments. It will also help if you take this book with you and write down some pre-prepared questions. There is a strong possibility you might forget some of your queries or be unable to absorb the answers. So, if you have someone else with you, they will be able to ask questions and better absorb the answers given by your healthcare providers.

When faced with the complexities of cancer, understanding your diagnosis is the first step towards recovery. That understanding starts with your healthcare team breaking down medical terminology into language that resonates with your personal experience. Conversations between you and your healthcare team form the basis of your cancer journey. Therefore, you must understand the conversation. Understanding starts with your questions, and the quality of your questions will determine the quality of the answers you receive.

The following are some questions you might consider asking your healthcare provider:

About your Cancer Diagnosis:

- What type and stage of cancer do I have?

- Can you explain the test report and what it means for my diagnosis?

- Are there any additional tests or scans needed to assess the extent of my cancer?

- What is the prognosis for my specific cancer type and stage?

- What are the treatment options available for my cancer, and what are their goals?

- What factors should I consider when deciding on a treatment plan?

- How will treatment decisions be made, and will I have a say in them?

- Are there any clinical trials or experimental treatments that might suit me?

- Is it advisable to seek a second opinion from another doctor or cancer specialist?

These questions are meant to provide a layman's understanding of cancer. The aim is for your healthcare provider to explain to you the specific characteristics, such as the stage, grade, and receptor status of the disease and which treatment options are available.

The answers to these questions demystify the diagnosis and give you the confidence to ask more in-depth questions. They empower you to actively engage with your healthcare rather than feeling like a bystander.

That information is the foundation upon which to base your treatment decisions. It will also aid you in communicating your diagnosis to your loved ones, ensuring they, too, fully understand the situation. Understanding your cancer in the context of your life enables you to navigate the choices ahead with clarity and confidence. That clarity is not just about the medical aspects of your cancer but also about recognising the personal impact it will have on your life in the future.

Treatment and Care Options:

- What are the potential benefits and risks of each treatment option?

- How will treatment affect my daily life, including work, family, and social activities?

- What are the recommended treatments' expected side effects, and how do I manage them?

- How often will I need treatment, and what is the schedule?

- Will I require surgery, radiation therapy, chemotherapy, immunotherapy, targeted therapy, or a combination of treatments?

- Are there alternative or complementary therapies that may support my treatment plan?

- How should I prepare for treatment, and are there any lifestyle changes I should consider?

These questions start a discussion about the range of treatments tailored to your specific type and stage of cancer. The questions will provide answers regarding the range of treatments available to you. That could be surgery, radiation therapy, chemotherapy, immunotherapy, or targeted treatments. You might be offered the option of participating in clinical trials, which provide access to

The questions will provide answers regarding the range of treatments available to you. That could be surgery, radiation therapy, chemotherapy, immunotherapy, or targeted treatments

cutting-edge therapies. The line of questioning aims to ensure each treatment option is outlined in clear and straightforward terms. The information also outlines how the treatment will be carried out, how it fights cancer, and its availability, given your current state of health.

You must have clarity about whether the treatment is curative or palliative. Curative treatment aims to completely eradicate the cancer, while palliative treatment relieves the symptoms and improves your quality of life. Surgeons can remove many cancers in the early stages. Others require more aggressive treatments such as chemotherapy, radiation or a combination with the goal of remission. Such therapies are considered curative. On the other hand, the aim of some treatments is simply to shrink the cancer, slow its growth, prevent it from spreading and reduce the severity of the symptoms. Those are palliative or control-focused treatments.

How to Evaluate Treatment Options:

When evaluating treatment options, you must consider the potential outcomes, the probability of success, and the possible side effects. Each treatment option has a specific objective: curative, control, or symptom alleviation. The consideration must balance the aggressive management of the disease and the preservation of quality of life.

Furthermore, every treatment comes with its potential benefits and risks. It's essential to study the benefits and risks of each treatment carefully. You need a thorough understanding of each treatment's side effects to decide if you are prepared to endure them. Some treatments might severely impact your daily routines and long-term health. Some may require significant time commitment, frequent doctor visits, or disruptive recovery periods and lead to long-term health risks, such as secondary cancers, heart disease, kidney or fertility issues. Therefore, you must clearly understand the impact of treatment options on your life and lifestyle.

Follow-Up and Monitoring

- What is the schedule for follow-up appointments and surveillance after cancer treatment?
- What signs or symptoms should I watch for, and when should I contact you or seek emergency care?

The regularity with which you will visit your doctor for post-cancer treatment depends primarily on the type and stage of the cancer you had, the treatments you received, and your overall health. It would be best to question your doctor about post-treatment care at the beginning. Awareness of the post-treatment care for each treatment will enable you to decide on the treatment option that also considers your individual dynamic. Post-cancer visits usually involve physical examinations, blood tests, or imaging studies to indicate changes in your health. They also allow you to discuss any ongoing symptoms or concerns you may have.

Follow-up visits also allow you to discuss any lingering physiological or psychological side effects of treatment. They help assess your ability to cope with life after cancer treatment and ensure you are receiving the best support. The discussions could also include referrals to rehabilitation, mental health professionals, and a dietician.

Support and Survivorship

- What resources are available to help me cope with the emotional and psychological aspects of cancer?
- Are there support groups, counselling services, or survivorship programmes I can join?
- How can I manage my financial challenges during treatment?
- What are the long-term effects (late effects) of my cancer treatment, and how will they be monitored?
- Can you give me information on survivorship care plans and follow-up care after treatment?
- How can I maintain a healthy lifestyle, including diet and exercise, during and after cancer treatment?
- How will my cancer affect my ability to work, and is there legal and financial support available?
- What should I know about insurance coverage (for private patients) for my cancer treatment, including costs and details?
- Are there local or national cancer organisations that can assist me with financial or logistical challenges?

Cancer can be incredibly challenging if you cannot cope with the day-to-day necessities of life. Therefore, asking your healthcare provider to point you towards help for practical matters makes sense. Please do not assume that the practical issues have nothing to do with your healthcare provider, or they may not know the answer. Every healthcare facility has departments for handling non-clinical matters that affect patient treatment. So, ask them for help. In upcoming chapters, I outline several channels you could explore for help regarding non-clinical issues. However, in your initial meeting, ensure you include them in your questions to your healthcare provider.

Please remember that open and honest communication with your healthcare provider is critical for your recovery. Please remember to write down your questions before your appointments and take along a trusted friend or family member for support. You or your support person must take notes during the discussions to help you remember the information provided.

You can also ask your oncologist (cancer doctor) if it is okay to record the session. That way, you can have a taped recording of the answers to your questions.

ACTION PLAN

Step-by-Step Questions to Ask About Your Diagnosis

Step 1

Ask your healthcare provider to provide you with a clear explanation of your cancer type, stage, and grade.

Step 2

Ask about the key characteristics of your cancer and how they may affect the prognosis and treatment.

Step 3

Ask about ALL the treatment options available for your type and stage of cancer.

Step 4

Ask for an explanation of the goals of each treatment option.

Step 5

Ask about both the short-term and long-term side effects of the proposed treatments.

Step 6

Ask about how the side effects could affect your daily life and long-term health.

Step 7

Ask about the frequency and nature of follow-up visits and what will be involved.

Step 8

Ask about logistical help when undergoing treatment and during follow-up sessions.

Step 9

Ask about support systems, support groups and community organisations.

____

____

Chapter Three: Your Cancer Diagnosis in Layman's Language

Often, cancer diagnoses are laden with complex medical terminologies that are difficult for the average person to understand. Cancer diagnosis is the start of a voyage through uncharted waters. While the path may be strewn with challenges, understanding your diagnosis, and making early preparations can smooth it out. Understanding your diagnosis helps you clarify its medical specifics and make informed decisions. It provides a semblance of control in an otherwise tumultuous and confusing situation.

Each term holds critical implications for treatment and prognosis. Therefore, demystifying the terminology aids in constructing a clearer picture of the journey ahead. This knowledge is a vital step in transitioning from a passive recipient of instructions from your doctor to becoming an informed, active participant in your care.

To acquire the requisite knowledge to understand your cancer diagnosis, do the following:

Gain Awareness: Take time to learn about your diagnosis and treatment options. Knowledge is power and a critical factor in making informed decisions.

Ask Questions: Realise this is a new domain for you. So, it would be best to ask your healthcare provider clarifying questions. Do not view questioning them as being obstructive. The better your understanding, the higher your probability of actively participating in decision-making about your treatment.

Seek Specificity: Seek to understand the specific type of cancer you have. Is it a carcinoma, sarcoma, leukaemia, or lymphoma? Each behaves differently and has different treatment protocols.

Know the Stage of Your Cancer: Your cancer stage provides information on how far it has progressed. I outline the stages below, but they range from one to four and are determined by size, lymph node involvement, and whether the cancer has spread.

Question Your Treatment Options: You must review the various treatment options with your healthcare provider and discuss the benefits, risks, and impacts on your quality of life. That will help you make an informed decision about your treatment.

Request a Second Opinion: Deciding about something as complex as cancer treatment requires accurate information. Therefore, it is best to seek a second opinion before reaching your final decision. Discussing that possibility with your healthcare provider in your first appointment is essential.

Breakdown the Information: it's crucial you break down the information into its components to understand it better. Based upon that, you and your healthcare provider will develop a treatment plan that aligns with your personal health goals and values.

What is Cancer?

The simplest definition of cancer is the body's cells growing out of control. At its core, cancer is about cell behaviour. Our bodies are made up of trillions of cells. Typically, they grow and divide to form new cells as the body needs them. As cells become old or damaged, they die off, and new cells replace them. However, cancer interrupts this orderly process. Cells don't die when they should, and new cells form when the body doesn't need them. These extra cells then create a mass called a tumour.[15]

The following are some terms and phrases to help you understand the language surrounding cancer:

Cellular Growth and Division: Our bodies are made up of trillions of cells, each with a specific lifespan and function. Normal cells grow, divide, and die in an orderly fashion. Cancer disrupts this process, leading to uncontrolled cell growth.[16]

Mutation and Cancer Development: A mutation in a cell's DNA can cause it to become cancerous. These mutations may be random or caused by external factors such as cigarette smoke, radiation, or viruses.

Metastasis: When cancer cells break out of the primary tumour, they can travel through the bloodstream or lymphatic system to form new tumours. This process is known as metastasis. Metastasised cancer means the cancer has spread.

Benign and Malignant: These words describe the nature of a tumour. Benign tumours are non-cancerous. They are usually less risky. Malignant tumours are cancerous and can spread to other parts of the body.

Carcinoma: Refers to cancer that begins in the skin or organ tissue linings. It's the most common type of cancer.

Sarcoma: Sarcoma is a type of cancer originating in the bones or soft tissues like muscle and fat.

Leukaemia: Leukaemia is cancer of the blood-forming tissues, hindering the body's ability to produce healthy blood cells.

Lymphoma: Lymphoma is a cancer that begins in the lymphatic system, the disease-fighting network throughout your body.

Oncologist: An oncologist is a doctor who specialises in treating cancer.[17]

Cancer Stages

Every cancer is defined by its origin or the type of cell that turned malignant. For instance, a breast carcinoma indicates that the cancer began in the cells lining the ducts or lobules of the breast.[18]

Knowing the stage of your cancer is crucial as it familiarises you with its size, depth, and whether it has spread.[19] That knowledge also helps your healthcare team give a prognosis, recommend treatments, and predict treatment success. The higher the stage, the more advanced the cancer.[20]

The stages of cancer are the following:

Stage 0: The cancer is localised. It has not spread to other body tissues. This stage is often called "in situ" or "pre-cancer."

Stages I-III: In stages one to three, the cancer is more extensive and has grown deeper into nearby tissues. It may have spread to nearby lymph nodes but not to other body parts.

Stage IV: Stage four cancer has spread to other parts of the body.

Tumour Grade refers to its aggressiveness. It provides insights into how the cancer cells are behaving. A high-grade tumour is aggressive, growing rapidly and spreading faster than a low-grade tumour.[21]

Understanding your cancer diagnosis enables you and your medical team to make the most appropriate treatment decisions. The treatment options for stage zero cancer are entirely different from the treatment options for stage four cancer. Therefore, you must understand your cancer diagnosis.

Understanding your pathology report

When you visit your oncologist, you undergo various tests, and they interpret the results for you. These tests are known as your pathology report. The information within the report guides the prognosis and treatment decisions for your cancer care.

Your pathology report contains the following information:

- The location in the body from where the specimen (tissue sample) was taken for testing and how the tissues were retrieved.

- A description of the specimen as seen by the naked eye. That includes the specimen's colour, weight, and size, any visible abnormalities, the number of samples taken, and information about any lymph nodes that were removed (if any were).
- A description of the specimen as seen under a microscope, including the type and number of cells in the tissue sample and how abnormal the cell looks, called the tumour grade, and a description of any notable cell features. The description notes whether the abnormal cells are in the edges of the tissues (margins) or your lymph nodes. Negative or clean margins indicate an absence of cancer cells at the edge of the tissue. Positive indicates the opposite, the presence of cancer cells at the edge of the tissue. The description might include positive or negative lymph nodes. Positive means the presence of cancer cells, and negative indicates the absence of cancer cells.
- A final diagnosis based on an assessment of the specimen by the naked eye and under the microscope. The pathologist will identify the type of cancer, the tumour grade (the abnormality of the cell), the status of the lymph node, the status of the margin, and the cancer stage.
- A comments section of the pathologist's report (not always present). The pathologist uses this section to give further details about the disease and suggest additional tests.[22]

Learn how to read the scans and various tests. Look out for words that suggest doubt and uncertainty, such as "might", "range from", "could", and "possibly".

Check whether the report suggests the tumour is "aggressive" or "slow-changing". An aggressive tumour means treatment must start immediately. In contrast, a slow-changing tumour means you have adequate time to decide on your treatment plan.

Check whether the report suggests the tumour is "aggressive" or "slow-changing". An aggressive tumour means treatment must start immediately. In contrast, a slow-changing tumour means you have adequate time to decide on your treatment plan

Check whether the cells are "poorly differentiated". If they are, you must get a second opinion because it is challenging to identify a specific cancer in poorly differentiated cells. Identifying the type of tumour is crucial because different tumours behave differently.

Part of understanding your cancer diagnosis is paying attention to the short and long-term consequences of your diagnosis.

Short-term Actions After A Cancer Diagnosis

When given a cancer diagnosis, there are short and long-term actions you need to take. Focus on the following short-term actions:

Diagnosis Verification: Ensure the diagnosis is accurate. Request detailed information about your diagnosis using the questions in Chapter Two. Ask for the scan and biopsy results and request an explanation of them.

Decide on Your Treatment Options: As you read above, the goal of your cancer treatment could be curative or palliative. You must settle on that with your healthcare provider.

Managing Symptoms: Ask questions about potential side effects of treatments to prepare adequately for them. Some side effects, such as fatigue, nausea, mood changes or cognitive malfunctions, can impact your daily routines. Another thing you might want to be aware of is pain. It would be best if you made provisions for pain management.

Support Your Overall Health: request a comprehensive evaluation of your health to understand how your current health may influence treatment options and outcomes. Your body has to be in the best possible condition to handle specific cancer treatments, or you may be unable to tolerate them.

In addition to the short-term impacts of cancer treatment, there are also long-term consequences. The long-term effects are not just physiological. There are also emotional and psychological aspects of living as a cancer survivor. Understanding these is key to developing a comprehensive recovery and survivorship care plan.

Please consider the following potential long-term impacts:

Chronic Side Effects: Some treatments may result in persistent side effects such as fatigue, neuropathy, or cognitive changes, impacting daily living.

Secondary Health Risks: There are risks of developing secondary health problems or even secondary cancers requiring ongoing monitoring and preventive care.

Physical Rehabilitation: Long-term recovery may involve rehabilitation to restore compromised strength, mobility, and functionality.

Lifestyle changes: Lifestyle changes, including diet, exercise, and mental health support, are critical for enhancing long-term recovery.

Follow-up Checks: Regular post-treatment screenings and check-ups are imperative to preventing cancer recurrence and promptly addressing side effects and other concerns.

As you adapt to your new reality, you must educate yourself about the nuances of cancer. Education is a pillar of empowerment that illuminates your path to effective management and recovery from the disease. Knowledge is a source of strength, enabling you to make informed decisions and take control of your journey.

The following are some things you should pay particular attention to:

Study Cancer

Develop your understanding of cancer by learning its biology, treatment options, and the potential side effects of various treatments. That will help you have informed conversations with your oncologist and other healthcare professionals.

Stay Current

Keep yourself abreast of the latest research and advancements in cancer treatment. That could require subscribing to newsletters from reputable cancer research institutions or attending educational seminars. You should also join cancer network groups.

Informed Treatment Choice

The more you understand cancer, the better position you are in to make informed decisions about your treatment plans. Understanding the rationale behind treatment recommendations from your healthcare providers helps you make decisions that align with your values and lifestyle.

Become Your Own Advocate

Being educated about your cancer diagnosis helps you to advocate on your own behalf when interacting with your healthcare provider. That ensures your preferences and values are respected.

Where to Access Information

Use trusted sources like the National Cancer Institute, the American Cancer Society in the US, or Cancer Research UK and Macmillan Cancer Support if you live in the UK. These organisations offer credible information.

Collaborate With Your Healthcare Team

Your oncologist is your first source of credible information. The rest of your healthcare team is your second source of reliable information. So, collaborate with them, clarify the terminologies you struggle to understand, and ensure they explain your treatment plan in layperson's language.

Learn from Other Cancer Patients

Get involved with cancer support groups to learn from the experiences of others facing similar challenges. There is no better education than getting it directly from someone with actual experience.

Educate your Family and Friends

Be prepared to be your loved ones' teacher. There is a good chance they know almost nothing about cancer. So, be a patient teacher to ensure they understand and support you effectively.

ACTION PLAN

Step 1

Ensure you request detailed information about the specific type and stage of your cancer from your healthcare provider.

Step 2

Obtain copies of your medical reports and ask your healthcare provider to point out and explain detailed information in the report.

Step 3

Conduct research into your type of cancer using reputable sources.

Step 4

Learn the biology and characteristics of cancer, common terminologies, and treatment options.

Step 5

Learn about the goal and potential outcomes of each treatment.

Step 6

Ensure you understand the side effects of treatments and how they might impact your quality of life.

Step 7

Consider the impact of your treatment options on your daily life and long-term goals.

Step 8

Before agreeing to a treatment plan, seek a second opinion and explore all possible options.

Step 9

Discuss your diagnosis and treatment with family and friends and ask for suggestions.

Step 10

Get involved with support groups, either locally or online, for emotional support.

Step 11

Keep up to date with the latest research or advancements in treatment for your type of cancer.

Step 12

Subscribe to newsletters or alerts for cancer information.

Chapter Four: How to Request a Second Opinion

Different oncologists might read a pathology report and produce differing opinions on the type, stage, and proposed treatment for your cancer.

> While the exact number of cancers misdiagnosed cases is unknown, Larry Martel, in his book *Embracing Cancer—Embracing Life: The Guide for the Journey Beyond Diagnosis,* suggests that 15% of all cancers in the US are misdiagnosed. John Hopkins Hospital found that 1.4% of its diagnoses were incorrect.[23]

A cancer diagnosis can be overwhelming. While the trust we place in our medical team is well-founded, seeking a second opinion is a practical and sometimes necessary step. It could offer you and your medical team invaluable insights.

A second opinion is when you consult or seek an additional assessment. It is a fundamental component of informed medical decision-making and could enhance the quality of your care. Second opinions are not a sign of mistrust or disrespect. They are a collaborative approach to diagnosis and treatment.

So, consult another oncologist, medical specialist, or healthcare institution to validate or supplement the initial diagnosis and treatment plan. That process ensures you receive the most accurate and appropriate care for your cancer.

The Value of a Second Opinion

There are always situations when you visit your healthcare provider you will have questions about your diagnosis, prognosis, treatment, or medication. Never be afraid to ask and don't hesitate to request a second opinion. Healthcare professionals, regardless of their education or experience, are humans therefore, liable to make mistakes. Remember that healthcare professionals are always practicing. Requesting a second opinion does not mean you doubt your doctor's capabilities. You are simply seeking the best treatment for you.

The reality is that medical error is an ongoing situation. An eight-year study released by John Hopkins Hospital in 2016 reported that for each of those eight years, over 250,000 people in the US died as a result of medical error. Making medical error the third leading cause of death in the US.[24] That is over 250,000 people dying from medical errors each year. Medical error is the "failure of a planned action to be completed as intended or using a wrong plan to achieve an aim". A medical error resulting in medical injury is a preventable adverse event. An adverse event is "an injury caused by medical management rather than by the underlying disease or condition of the patient".[25]

When to Request a Second Opinion

Request a second opinion if you are in any of the following situations:

- Your pathology test results do not define the type of cancer you have.
- Your pathology test results do not specify the stage of your cancer.
- You are uncomfortable with the diagnosis.
- You feel the need to have another oncologist confirm what your current oncologist has said regarding your illness.
- You believe your oncologist has failed to consider something important when making their diagnosis.
- You desire more comprehensive information about a proposed course of treatment suggested by your oncologist. You want to know all the risks, side effects, toxicity, and impacts on your ability to work, reproduce, etc.
- Your oncologist has proposed several treatment options, and you are unsure which to choose.
- You want to speak to an oncologist who is more open to alternative treatments or newer treatment options.
- Your oncologist has suggested a deviation from your current therapy or complementing additional treatment.
- Your cancer is rare, and not much information is available about it.
- Your oncologist is inexperienced in treating your type of cancer.

- Your oncologist does not seem to regard your opinion or appears frustrated with your questions or questioning.
- Your oncologist does not communicate effectively in a way that you can understand.
- You propose the idea of becoming a clinical trial candidate, and your oncologist flatly rejects such an idea, insisting the standard treatment is best.
- Your oncologist negatively reacts to you informing them of your desire for a second opinion.

Another key reason for seeking a second opinion is recognising that patient needs might differ. Each patient is unique, and cancer itself exhibits a wide range of variations in terms of type, stage, and genetic characteristics. Consequently, the insights of multiple medical professionals can significantly contribute to a comprehensive understanding of the disease and an individualised treatment plan.

In a study published in The Oncologist, researchers found that second opinions often lead to changes in the initial diagnosis and treatment plan, demonstrating the potential for improved patient outcomes.[26] These changes could include refining the diagnosis, adjusting the cancer stage, or recommending an alternative treatment plan. Sometimes, a second opinion may offer a more optimistic outlook, providing hope and relief to patients and their families.

Numerous studies suggest that a second opinion can confirm or provide alternative treatment options. An assessment of 25 studies revealed that up to 88% of patients seeking a second opinion left with a refined or new diagnosis.[27] Another

Another study published in The Oncologist found that approximately 20% of patients who sought second opinions received a different diagnosis or experienced a significant change in their treatment plan.

study published in The Oncologist found that approximately 20% of patients who sought second opinions received a different diagnosis or experienced a significant change in their treatment plan.[28] These changes often led to more tailored and effective treatment approaches.

Furthermore, medical professionals, like all other professionals, are fallible. They could misinterpret the scan report or overlook certain aspects of the report that another medical professional could pick up.

Second Opinion Myths and Misconceptions

Several myths and misconceptions surround the quest for a second opinion. The reluctance to seek a second opinion often stems from the misconception that it shows mistrust in your healthcare provider, which might offend them.

However, you must recognise that medical professionals anticipate and respect your right to second opinions. They understand its value. Requesting a second opinion is proactive involvement in your treatment.

Myth One: A request for a second opinion offends your primary healthcare team

This is probably the most common misconception. However, healthcare professionals are accustomed to patients requesting second opinions. So, they are rarely offended. Most healthcare professionals consider such requests a valuable aspect of collaborative care. Effective communication helps alleviate concerns and maintains a positive relationship with your healthcare team.

Myth Two: Second opinions are time-consuming, which delays treatment.

Some people worry that seeking a second opinion will lead to significant delays in their treatment. While making informed decisions promptly is essential, you can manage to get a second opinion efficiently. Healthcare providers recognise the urgency of addressing cancer cases and prioritise second opinions.

Myth Three: Second opinions are costly.

Financial considerations are another barrier to second opinions. However, many insurance plans cover the cost. Additionally, resources are available to assist patients facing financial obstacles. Being accustomed to free healthcare, many Brits might cringe at the idea of paying for medical treatment. They are convinced it's costly. However, diagnostic care in the UK is not as expensive as you might think. It's not the purview of the rich. Most ordinary folks can afford it. Private treatment is out of reach for most people, but most people can afford a diagnosis. Besides, it is expensive compared to what? What is the cost of being given the wrong diagnosis? Please remember also that some charities cover the cost of a second opinion.

You must understand that the critical reason for requesting a second opinion is for diagnostic confirmation. Cancer diagnoses are complex and rely on combining clinical evaluations, imaging, and pathological assessments. While oncologists strive for accuracy, diagnostic errors occur due to complexity and various interpretations.

How to Seek Second Opinion in the UK

According to Dr Fitzgerald, you should get a second opinion after your pathology report and before commencing any form of treatment.[29]

In England and Wales, you have the right to request a second opinion when you receive a diagnosis from your GP or consultant. The NHS allows patients to choose which doctor or clinical team they want to see.

Your general practitioner who suspects a cancer diagnosis will send you to a hospital. That hospital will send you to a cancer specialist (oncologist). You might find your request for a second opinion rejected, or if accepted, you might disagree with the choice of specialist. In either situation, you can independently source and pay your preferred oncologist. The initial consultation fee will cost you approximately **£200.**[30]

If your cancer is aggressive and you are denied a second opinion, you have the choice to pay out of pocket and potentially save your life.

If you have private insurance, you can choose your primary oncologist and source a second opinion.

Additional information for residents of Wales

You can get access to a second opinion from specialists like oncologists through your GP, who will refer you to the most qualified specialist in your area. You must first obtain a referral letter.

If you still desire a second opinion from a private specialist, you must get a referral from your GP. If you visit a private specialist without a referral, your GP is not obliged to accept the advice offered.

If you experience trouble getting a second opinion, you can find contact information for your seven new health boards at https://111.wales.nhs.uk/localservices/localhealthboards/

OR

Seek advice from your local Community Health Council. You can visit the website https://111.wales.nhs.uk/localservices/communityhealthcouncils/ to find details on how to contact the seven community health councils.

OR

Seek advice from your local Citizens Advice Bureau. You can make contact with them through their website https://www.citizensadvice.org.uk/wales/

In Scotland, you can request your GP to refer you for a second opinion. If the GP disagrees, they must provide a valid reason.

Additional information for residents of Northern Ireland

In Northern Ireland, you can make a request of your GP or consultant to refer you for a second opinion. That request is usually granted unless there are compelling reasons against it.

If you have issues getting a referral for a second opinion, get advice from the Patient Advisory & Liaison Service at the hospital where you receive treatment.

Or

Contact a specialist nurse at a Daffodil Centre by email via supportline@irishcancer.ie or by phone on their support line at 1800 200 700.[31]

Or

Visit a Daffodil Centre based in a hospital nearest you for support information by visiting https://www.cancer.ie/cancer-information-and-support/cancer-support/find-support/daffodil-centres#locations

In the United States, you can ask your primary doctor or insurance company to refer you for a second opinion. In fact, some insurance plans require a second opinion. Otherwise, if a referral is unnecessary, you can seek a second opinion by contacting another oncologist.

Steps for Requesting a Second Opinion in the UK

Step One: Discuss the situation with your GP or oncologist

Talk with your GP or oncologist about your intention to seek a second opinion. Be transparent and open. You might be surprised. They could recommend specialists or medical facilities. Also, conduct extensive research into specialists in your area. These days, you can contact specialists from any part of the globe.

Step Two: Choose a specialist or hospital

Based on your research and recommendations from your GP or oncologist, select a specialist or hospital and contact them. Consider things such as the specialist's expertise, location, and the healthcare facility's reputation.

Step Three: Obtain Referral from Your GP or Oncologist

You will require a referral from your GP or oncologist to see another specialist. Therefore, you need to be open about your desire.

Step Four: Make an Appointment

Once you have settled on the specialist or medical facility you want to visit, contact them and schedule an appointment. Ensure you have your complete medical records, including your initial diagnosis and test results.

Step Five: Attend the Appointment

Attend the appointment and discuss your case with the specialist. They will review your medical history, conduct examinations, and provide their assessment and recommendations. Ensure you have a list of questions ready, and don't go there alone. Take a friend, loved one or support worker.

Step Six: Share the second opinion with your primary doctor.

After the appointment, share the findings and recommendations with your primary oncologist. The information could alter your diagnosis and treatment plan.

A Step-by-Step Guide for Requesting a Second Opinion in the United States

Obtaining a second opinion in the United States is common. Patients can autonomously seek multiple medical opinions. Take the following steps:

Step One: Advise your primary physician.

Communicate your intention to your primary physician or oncologist. They can recommend specialists or medical facilities catering to your specific cancer diagnosis.

Step Two: Research and choose a specialist.

Research and identify a specialist or medical facility specialising in your type of cancer. Things to consider include the specialist's reputation, location, and accessibility.

You can access hundreds of oncologists in the United States at https://health.usnews.com/doctors/oncologists

Step Three: Schedule an appointment

Schedule an appointment and gather your medical records, test results and other relevant information.

Step Four: Attend the Appointment

During your consultation, the specialist will review your medical history, conduct assessments, and offer expert opinions and treatment recommendations. Take your list of questions with you, and do not attend the appointment alone. Take a friend or loved one with you.

Step Five: Share the report with your primary physician.

Share the findings and recommendations with your primary physician. The information may prompt them to change their diagnosis or treatment plan.

Telemedicine Medicine Makes Second Opinion Easier

The advancement of telemedicine has changed the way we seek second opinions. You can consult specialists remotely, eliminating geographical barriers. That is especially valuable when transport might be challenging for health, logistical, or financial reasons.

Here are some ways telemedicine makes obtaining a second opinion easier:

Accessibility: Telemedicine makes second opinions accessible to and from anywhere.

Efficiency: It is virtual, so you can schedule appointments quickly.

Expertise: You have access to world-renowned experts.

Medical Records: You can securely share your medical records, scans and test results.

Collaboration: The specialist can efficiently liaise with your primary physicians and specialists, ensuring a coordinated approach.

ACTION PLAN

Step 1

Be aware that you have a right to a second opinion, a common and supported healthcare practice.

Step 2

Request a complete copy of your medical records, including tests, scans, and lab results from your doctor.

Step 3

Research specialists experienced in your type of cancer. Consider teaching hospitals or specialist cancer centres known for researching and treating your specific cancer type.

Step 4

Contact your insurance company to verify coverage for a second opinion and ask them about specific procedures or specialists that are in-network.

Step 5

Note your questions about your diagnosis, prognosis and treatment options. Prepare a summary of your health history and symptoms.

Step 6

Ask your doctor for a referral to a specialist he knows or contact cancer advocacy groups for recommendations.

Step 7

Contact the specialist's office to schedule an appointment. Explain to the receptionist that you seek a second opinion on your diagnosis and treatment plan.

Step 8

Take all your medical records and the list of questions to the appointment. Go accompanied and take notes.

Step 9

After the appointment, review the specialist's feedback and compare it with your initial diagnosis and treatment plan.

Step 10

Take time to consider the information and opinions you've received. Reflect on how they align with your goals and values.

Step 11

Discuss the second opinion with your primary healthcare provider. Open communication helps ensure they consider treatment options.

Step 12

Use the insights from the second opinion to make an informed decision about your treatment plan.

Step 13

If you decide to change your treatment plan based on the second opinion, follow up with your necessary healthcare providers and implement the changes.

Step 14

Consider speaking with a patient navigator or counsellor to help process the information and support your decision-making process.

Step 15

Whichever direction your treatment takes, continue with regular follow-ups and remain proactive.

Each step helps ensure you feel informed, respected, and in control of your healthcare decisions.

Available Resources

Numerous platforms connect patients with specialist medical doctors worldwide. Platforms like the Second Opinion Expert in the US or Best Doctors in the UK provide online medical consultations.

Chapter Five: Understanding Your Treatment Options

Cancer remains a dreaded word because information about treatment is still not widely available. Granted, cancer treatments remain brutal. However, the recovery rate is extremely high. What is missing is knowledge about the most appropriate treatments.

What to Consider When Making Cancer Treatment Decision

Being asked by an oncologist who has been working with cancer for decades to choose a treatment option can be challenging, especially when dealing with the emotions involved with such a diagnosis.

Please consider the following factors when deciding on your most appropriate treatment option:

Stage of your Cancer:

In most instances, early-stage cancers only require surgery. However, advanced-stage cancers often require a combination of treatments. For example, stage 1 breast cancer might require a surgical operation in which the surgeon removes a lump from the breast. Stages 3 or 4 breast cancer might require chemotherapy, radiation, and targeted therapy. Your doctor can advise you on the best treatment option. However, you should know why they have chosen specific treatment options.

Your Age and General Health

Your age and overall health are crucial when determining your treatment. The younger you are, the more capable you are of handling aggressive treatment. The older you are, the less likely you can tolerate specific therapies. Furthermore, the sicker you are, the less likely you are to cope with some treatments.

Geographical Considerations

Your place of residence also determines your accessibility to specific treatments. In the UK, it's called the treatment postcode lottery. The most advanced cancer treatments are in London. We can say the same about the US. The most advanced cancer treatments are in cities with advanced research universities and facilities.

Cancer Treatment Options:

Chemotherapy for cancer treatment

Chemotherapy was established as the preeminent cancer treatment in the 1940s.[32] Chemotherapy consists of different drugs that inhibit cell growth. Each targets different cell growth phases, ensuring comprehensive coverage. While highly potent against rapidly growing cancer cells, the drugs also inadvertently destroy healthy cells.

Chemotherapy can be given intravenously (through your veins) or as tablets (oral chemotherapy), which the doctor prescribes for you to take at home.[33]

How and when is chemotherapy used?

Oncologists typically recommend chemotherapy if:

- your cancer has spread or is likely to spread,
- it will decrease the risk of cancer returning after surgery or radiotherapy,
- to help patients manage symptoms in cases where a cancer cure is impossible. This treatment is called palliative chemotherapy.

Chemotherapy can be used to achieve a complete cancer cure.

Chemotherapy can also be combined with surgery, as mentioned above. This type of treatment is called neoadjuvant chemotherapy.

Oncologists also combine chemotherapy with radiotherapy, termed chemoradiation.

Chemotherapy drugs include:

Plant Alkaloids

Plant Alkaloids come from specific types of plants. They are cell-cycle-specific agents, like taxanes, derived from the Pacific yew tree. They prevent cell division and are primarily used for breast, ovarian, and lung cancers.

Topoisomerase Inhibitors

Topoisomerase inhibitors prevent the action of topoisomerase enzymes, which help separate the DNA strands so they can be copied. These include drugs such as irinotecan and etoposide.

Antitumor Antibiotics

Antitumor Antibiotics prevent enzymes involved in DNA replication from replicating. An example of this drug is Doxorubicin, which treats many different cancers.

As with many medications, there are side effects that you may experience. These depend on the type and location of your cancer, the drug and its dosage, and your overall health.

The following are the most common chemotherapy side effects:

- you are more susceptible to infection,
- a feeling of being unwell,
- hair loss,
- dry, sore, or itchy skin,
- diarrhea,
- constipation,
- weariness.[34]

Other side effects include problems with the nervous system (brain and spinal cord CNS) or peripheral nervous system (PNS).

How Chemotherapy Might Impact Your CNS

You might have memory problems or experience difficulty solving problems and calculations. You could lose your sense of balance and experience dizziness, nausea, and vertigo. Vertigo leaves you feeling like the room is spinning. You may also have coordination problems and seizures.

How chemotherapy might impact your PNS

You might feel weak all the time, feeling you don't have the strength to walk or coordinate yourself. Your hands and feet might burn, or you may get a tingling sensation in them. You might not be able to control your urination. If you are a male, you may experience erectile dysfunction.

You might have issues with your hearing and experience tinnitus (ringing ears). You could have blurred or double vision or experience vision loss. You might not be able to taste and smell as usual or experience difficulty swallowing. You could also experience slurred speech or difficulty understanding when others are speaking.

Chemotherapy drugs that might lead to CNS side effects:

- Drugs classed as vinca alkaloids. These include vincristine, vinorelbie, and vinblastine.
- Platinum-based drugs like cisplatin or oxaliplatin.
- Taxane drugs like docetaxel and paclitaxel.
- Etoposide
- High doses of cytarabine
- High doses of ifosfamide

- High doses of methotrexate

Other causes of CNS side effects from chemotherapy

Side effects will most likely occur when:

- cancers are located in the brain or spine,
- chemo drugs are injected into your spine,
- nerves are damaged during surgery,
- you have undergone radiotherapy to the brain and/or spine.

How to manage CNS side effects

Your healthcare provider might prescribe medicines for side effects, antibiotics to remedy infections and corticosteroids to minimize inflammation and swelling. However, as always, the medications themselves can cause other side effects. It is always necessary to discuss these with your healthcare provider and do your own checks on any drugs before you are prescribed. There are always alternative options. When the side effects cause you pain and discomfort, you have the option of using opioids and nerve blockers. You may also access rehabilitation health professionals when you have lost independence or physical strength.[35]

Radiation therapy for cancer treatment

Radiation Therapy, also known as radiotherapy, involves using "high doses of radiation to kill cancer cells and shrink tumours". The cancer cells die when the high-dose radiation damages their DNA, making it impossible for them to divide. They do not die immediately. Days or weeks of treatment are needed for the radiation to damage the cancer cell's DNA to the point where it dies. The cell death then happens over weeks or months. Dead cells are then broken down and removed from the body.

Types of radiation therapy includes:

- 3D-CRT: Three-dimensional conformal radiation therapy allows radiation to conform to the cancer's shape, reducing damage to healthy tissues.
- IGRT: Image-guided radiation therapy offers real-time imaging to guide radiation delivery. That also ensures the beam only targets the cancer, not the surrounding tissues.
- Proton Therapy: Proton therapy is an advanced radiation therapy that targets tumours with protons instead of x-rays, minimizing damage to surrounding healthy tissue.

Types of radiation therapy

You will encounter two types of radiotherapy: external beam and internal beam. As the name suggests, external beam radiation therapy attacks cancer from outside your body. A large machine aims radiation at the part of your body that has the tumour without actually touching you.[36] It is administered daily over several weeks, but some cancers may require treatment multiple times per day. Though the radiation targets the tumour, it impacts normal tissues as it passes in and out of your body. Smaller doses called fractions are given over several weeks until they add up to the intended gray to limit the damage to normal tissues. The amount of radiation is measured in gray. Depending on your cancer type and size, you could receive multiple doses per day. Hyperfractioned radiation splits the dosage into two sessions, but the treatment length is unaltered. Accelerated radiation involves administrating the total dosage over a shorter period. Hypofractionated radiation involves administering the radiation in higher doses. These treatment schedules may prove suitable for some types of cancers. However, they often lead to early side effects, although later side effects are unaltered.[37]

Internal beam radiotherapy attacks the cancer from inside your body through a solid or liquid medium.

The solid medium is called brachytherapy. The radiation source is contained within a seed, ribbon, or capsule that is put inside the tumour or near the tumour inside your body. Because the source is placed near or on the tumour, there is less risk of damaging healthy tissues. The radiation source continues to emit radiation for some time.[38] This therapy is better for tumours that need high doses of radiation or when healthy tissues vulnerable to radiation are close to the cancer. Internal brachytherapy can make you a danger to other people while the implant remains in place.

Internal radiotherapy that uses a liquid source is called systemic radiation. The radiation source liquid is administered intravenously (injected into your vein) with a drip, via an injection or orally. The radiation accesses your tissues through your blood. As it travels through your blood, it seeks and kills cancer cells. Systemic radiation causes body fluids, such as saliva, sweat, and urine, to give off radiation for some time.[39]

Can radiation therapy cause a second cancer?

Radiation exposure can cause cancer within a 10 to 15-year period. Studies of the atomic bomb survivors in Japan have proven that. Furthermore, studies of people exposed to radiation at work and those who have undergone radiotherapy for cancer and other diseases show a link between radiation and cancer development.

Even leukaemia has been linked to previous exposure to radiation. Myelodysplastic syndrome (MDS), a cancer of the bone marrow that can transform into acute leukaemia, has also been linked to previous radiation exposure. Your risk of developing leukaemia after radiation exposure is dependent on the following:

a. how much of your bone marrow was exposed to radiation,

b. the amount of radiation that reached your bone marrow,

c. the radiation dosage rate (the amount and frequency of each dose and the time it took to take the dose).

Radiation therapy has also been linked to solid tumours like breast and lung cancer, which typically develop ten years or more after the first exposure. Your age, radiation dosage, and the area of your body treated with radiation determine second cancer development. The younger you are when exposed to radiation, the more likely you are to develop a solid tumour cancer. The higher the radiation dose, the more probable you will develop a second cancer later on. Second cancers usually develop in the treated area or near it. Breast and thyroid cancers seem to be more susceptible to second cancers when exposed to radiation therapy.[40]

Side effects of radiation treatment

The radiation used to kill or slow cancer growth in your body can damage healthy cells in the area surrounding the treatment target.

Brain

You will likely become very fatigued, experience hair loss, develop memory issues and have difficulty concentrating. You may also experience vomiting and nausea, headache and blurred vision. You may see changes in your skin,[41] such as dryness and itchiness. It could also turn red, darker, painful, wet, and become infected with sores.[42]

Breast

You will likely become fatigued, experience tenderness within your breast, hair loss and skin changes as noted above and swelling, commonly known as oedema, caused by a build-up of fluid in your tissues.

Chest

You will likely become fatigued, experience hair loss and skin changes, develop problems with your throat (difficulty swallowing), persistent coughing and shortness of breath.

Head and neck

You may experience fatigue, hair loss, mouth problems (sores, infections, swelling or pain, difficulty swallowing, and tooth decay), throat problems, and changes in how you experience taste.

Pelvis

You could become fatigued, experience hair loss, skin changes, sexual problems (both males and females may experience temporary loss of interest in sexual intercourse), fertility problems (both males and females, and it may be permanent[43]), nausea and vomiting, urinary and bladder problems (pain or burning when urinating, blood in urine, problems urinating, desiring to urinate often, leaking urine with each sneeze or cough, and cramp or discomfort in your pelvic area)

Rectum

You will probably become fatigued and experience hair loss, skin changes, diarrhoea, fertility and sex problems (both males and females), and urinary and bladder problems, as noted before.

Stomach and abdomen

You will probably experience fatigue, hair loss, skin changes, nausea and vomiting, diarrhoea, and urinary and bladder problems.

Modern radiation therapy targets cancer more precisely, and doctors have a better grasp of the correct doses.[44] Your side effects may diminish or end months after radiation treatment, but in some cases, they are permanent. You must decide if radiation treatment is for you or if you prefer another option.

Immunotherapy for cancer treatment

Immunotherapy is different from chemotherapy and radiotherapy. It uses substances created in a lab or those produced naturally by your body to boost your immune system, helping the body locate and eliminate cancer cells. Like with other treatment options for cancer, immunotherapy can be used in combination with other treatment options or by itself.

Usually, cancer eludes many of your immune system's natural defenses. Immunotherapy helps your immune system stop or slow cancer growth, destroy cancer cells, or prevent cancer from spreading.

Kinds of immunotherapy

Depending on your specific cancer, you can choose from different kinds of immunotherapy.

Monoclonal antibodies and immune checkpoint inhibitors

In response to threats, your immune system makes antibodies which attach to antigens. These antibodies are proteins that fight infections, and antigens are the enemies they fight. Laboratories prepare the monoclonal antibodies. The aim is to enhance your body's natural antibodies or to do the work of the antibodies themselves. Monoclonal antibodies block the work of abnormal proteins within cancer cells.

Monoclonal inhibitors deactivate immune checkpoints, preventing the immune system from attacking healthy cells.

Cancer usually evades your immune system by activating immune checkpoints, thus gaining freedom to roam. Immune checkpoint inhibitors include Atezolizumab (Tecentriq), Durvalumab (Imfinzi), and Pembrolizumab (Keytruda).[45] If you use monoclonal inhibitors, side effects include liver problems, fatigue, diarrhoea, skin rashes, and shortness of breath.[46]

Non-specific immunotherapies

Non-specific immunotherapies that include cytokines and bacillus calmette-guerin (BCG) help your immune system kill cancer cells.

Cytokines are natural messenger proteins that deliver messages between cells, telling them to activate the immune system.

Interferon is a cytokine the immune system produces, but laboratories can also manufacture it. Interferon proteins signal your body when a pathogen is detected and can also reduce the speed of cancer growth. Interferon is used for several cancer types. However, its side effects include skin rashes, hair thinning, flu-like symptoms, and increased exposure to infections.

Interleukins are another cytokine. They are also messenger proteins that initiate immune responses to pathogens. However, they can cause weight gain, low blood pressure, or flu-like symptoms.

BCG is used to treat bladder cancer where it is placed using a catheter. It attaches itself to the bladder lining and activates the immune system to kill cancer cells. However, it can cause flu-like symptoms.

Oncolytic virus therapy

This therapy uses lab-altered viruses to kill cancer cells. The virus is genetically modified and inserted into the tumour, where it multiplies, causing the cancer cells to burst and die. Proteins released from the dead cancer cells trigger your immune system to attack cancer cells with the same proteins the dead cancer cells released. Talimogene laherparepvec (Imlygic) or T-VEC is approved in the US to treat advanced melanoma that surgery cannot treat. Other oncolytic virus therapies are undergoing clinical trials.

T-cell therapy

With T-cell therapy, natural T-cells are removed from your blood, and receptor proteins are added, allowing them to recognize cancer cells. The T-cells are then reinserted into your body to seek out and kill cancer cells in the blood. However, the therapy can cause fever, low blood pressure and seizures.

Cancer vaccines

Vaccines are medicines that help your body fight disease by training your immune system to find and kill harmful pathogens. Cancer vaccines protect healthy people from developing certain types of cancers caused by viruses.[47]

Cancer vaccines expose your body to an antigen that alerts your immune system to kill it. One such cancer vaccine is Gardasil, which protects against the human papillomavirus (HPV).[48] However, HPV can cause cervical, vaginal, vulvar, and anal cancer. The hepatitis B vaccine can prevent you from becoming infected with hepatitis B, which can lead to liver cancer.

Cancer vaccines are available through clinical trials. However, the FDA has approved some for specific cancers. There are currently many clinical trials testing vaccines for bladder, breast, cervical, colorectal, kidney, lung, pancreatic, and prostate cancers, brain tumours, leukaemia, melanoma, and myeloma. You can ask your oncologist or general practitioner (GP) if you are eligible for a clinical trial based on your cancer type and stage and how you can sign up.

Cancer vaccines are less effective for older people who are sick and have a compromised or weak immune system or those with large tumours. In those cases, combining the cancer vaccine with other treatments is better.

Cancer vaccines also have to struggle against an immune system that your cancer has suppressed. Cancer cells develop from your own cells, so your immune system may not see them as harmful and ignore them.[49]

Immunotherapy Side Effects

With immunotherapy treatment, you may experience the following:

- chills and flu-like symptoms,
- fatigue,
- weight loss,
- constipation,
- diarrhoea,

- nausea and vomiting,
- coughing and shortness of breath,
- decreased appetite,
- headaches,
- injection-site pain,
- itching, rashes, and blisters,

Immunotherapy side effects can be temporary or permanent because the therapy alters the activity of immune system cells that remain in the body.[50]

How effective is immunotherapy against cancer?

Evidence suggests that only about 15% to 20% of cancer patients respond positively to immunotherapy. However, when it is effective, it results in miracles. Researchers do not yet know who will respond to immunotherapy because it is challenging to get patients for clinical trials; only about 3% of adult cancer patients sign up for them. Another problem with immunotherapy is its cost; it is very expensive.[51]

Surgery as cancer treatment

Surgery is the oldest form of cancer treatment. It remains the single most definitive treatment for many cancer types. Surgery has evolved dramatically from invasive to minimally invasive and robotic-assisted, reducing hospital stays and recovery time. Surgery involves removing the tumour and surrounding tissue. Healthcare providers predominantly uses surgery for stage 1 cancers.

Surgical procedures include the following:

Curative surgery completely removes the tumour and is effective in the early stages of cancer growth.

Palliative surgery relieves the symptoms but does not cure the cancer.

Preventive surgery removes tissue that doesn't have cancerous cells to prevent them from developing into a malignant tumour.

You can also undergo cancer surgery to assist your body in performing its normal functions. Sometimes, surgery is necessary to relieve cancer side effects. Healthcare providers also use surgery to determine if you have cancer, its location and whether it has metastasized (spread to other organs).

Before surgery, you will be anesthetised (given medicine to prevent you from feeling pain). After some surgeries, you can leave the hospital or clinic the same or the following day. This is termed outpatient surgery. When you have to stay in the hospital afterwards, it is called inpatient surgery.[52]

Recovering from cancer surgery at home

While at home, I encourage you to follow these guidelines to care for yourself, so you recover from your surgery as quickly as possible. If you have any doubts, please consult your healthcare provider. This information is general, not specific.

You must take care of your pain, scars, wounds, drains, and stomas. Be careful with your diet and self-care. You will need help with some daily activities.

Managing your pain

Be careful to take your prescribed pain medication on time. If you have side effects, contact your healthcare provider immediately. If your pain is still unbearable, contact your hospital's emergency department.

Caring for your wound

Follow your healthcare provider's instructions. Do not touch your wound with lotions or perfumes. Keep your dressings dry. Do not remove the stitches or staples; your healthcare provider will do that when the time comes. Do not touch or pick the scabs off of your wound.

Caring for your scar

Your surgical scar will change over time. Once it is healing, avoid sunlight exposure, which can worsen the scarring. Once your scar has fully healed (according to your surgeon), you can moisturise and massage it to alleviate pain and stiffness (ask your healthcare team for recommendation of the best moisturiser to use and how often).

Managing your drains and stomas

If you go home with a temporary drain or stoma, ensure you know how to care for it before you leave the hospital.

Conforming to a healthy diet

Eat natural foods rich in fibre, fat, and protein. Eat a balanced mix of fruits, vegetables, nuts, and grains. Drink plenty of water. Avoid ultra-processed, salty, spicy, and fatty foods. Do not drink alcohol or smoke.

Taking care of yourself

If you cannot bathe, use wet wipes or a sponge with mild soap. You may become constipated because of the pain medication. If this is the case, ask your healthcare provider to recommend a laxative. You may also encounter problems controlling your bladder or bowels; ask someone to help with a potty or getting you to the toilet if necessary.

Accomplishing daily activities

Do not worry about oversleeping. If you are tired and need to sleep, do so. Get someone to help with the household chores. Ask your healthcare provider about the activities to avoid, for example, sexual intercourse or driving. Try moderate movement and exercise (ask your healthcare provider for recommendations and when to begin).[53]

What to do if you are recuperating from cancer at a hospital/clinic

While recovering at a hospital or clinic, your healthcare provider should care for you. However, you should know what constitutes quality care to be able to assess the quality of your care. Remember, your life is at stake.

The following is a list of services you should expect from your healthcare providers:

- your nurse should record any symptoms that you inform them about,
- if your doctor make any change to your medication, your medical records need to be updated to reflect the change,
- the staff must check and clean your bandages and wounds according to the schedule in your file,
- your nurse must administer medications and treatments as directed by your file,
- your nurse must assist you with bathroom and hygiene-related care,
- your nurse must respond to your concerns about treatment, medication, and how you feel physically,
- your nurse must note any allergic reactions to your medication,
- your nurse must be able to perform tasks relating to your care effectively,
- your nurse must be able to operate any medical equipment used for your treatment,
- your nurse must monitor your health periodically,
- Your nurse must ensure that all equipment used for your care works correctly.[54]

Cancer Surgery Side Effects

The more complex the surgery, the greater the risk that comes with it. All surgeries have side effects, but your health-care provider can minimise them. Before surgery, the team should do the following:

- shave and clean the incision area to prevent infections,
- administer low-dose blood thinners to prevent blood clots.[55] A blood clot that cannot pass through a narrow passage is called an embolus. An embolus can cause a heart attack or stroke,[56]
- respiratory therapy to prevent pneumonia.

When you have cancer surgery, side effects can result from three things:

1. Surgery,
2. Drugs used during surgery,
3. The state of your health.

Ensuring the surgical team is competent, experienced, and have a good track record is a good idea. Question your surgical oncologist about his experience and the team he will use for your operation.

Get a list of the drugs used during your surgery and check their efficacy and side effects with your doctor or surgeon. Research them yourself and ask if there are alternatives if you are uncomfortable with the answers. A reliable place to check the efficacy and side effects of drugs is https://www.drugs.com/

The state of your physical and mental health impacts how you fare during and after surgery. It is essential to inform your doctor of every illness and try to eliminate stress or mental anguish before surgery. Make the lifestyle and dietary changes mentioned in this handbook. The healthier your immune system when you go into surgery, the greater your chances of a smooth recovery with fewer side effects.

The following are side-effects you are likely to experience:

Pain

The incision point will be painful. Luckily, there are many painkillers available. Your surgeon will prescribe them but check their side effects. Ask your healthcare team and check https://www.drugs.com/. If uncomfortable, ask for alternatives.

Infection

Another common side effect after surgery is infection at the incision point.[57] Infections can be life-threatening and delay recovery. Keep a vigilant eye on the medical team attending you. Ensure they wash their hands and wear masks and gloves when they should. Ensure they keep your incision clean and dressed.

Help yourself by washing often, keeping the dressing clean and dry, and eating healthily. Avoid smoking or applying anything to the wound unless instructed by your medical team. Take the recommended medicine (unless side effects are harmful. In that case, contact your medical team immediately and ask for an alternative).[58]

Bleeding

You might have internal and external postoperative bleeding. Internal bleeding is more insidious because you can't see it. Internal bleeding can result from an unsealed blood vessel or a wound opening because of unsecured stitches.[59] Bleeding can be caused by damage to organs, liver or kidney disease, or a bleeding disorder. Blood thinners like aspirin, vitamins, and herbal supplements that impact blood clotting can cause bleeding.

You will know if you are bleeding if you see blood soaking through your bandages. If the bleeding is internal, you might detect it because you urinate less or not at all, breathe faster than usual, experience shortness of breath, have a faster heart rate, or are confused or anxious

You will know if you are bleeding if you see blood soaking through your bandages. If the bleeding is internal, you might detect it because you urinate less or not at all, breathe faster than usual, experience shortness of breath, have a faster heart rate, or are confused or anxious.

To confirm internal bleeding, your medical team might test your blood.

If bleeding is confirmed, you might need another surgery, an endoscopy or angiography to determine the source. Corrective measures include blood transfusions with components such as platelets or plasma to help your blood clot. Alternatively, you may be given antifibrinolytic medicines to slow or stop your bleeding.[60]

Blood clots

If you lie in bed too much, blood clots may occur in the legs. To avoid or minimise this, you are encouraged to move your legs by sitting, standing, and walking as soon as possible. A blood clot in the leg can be deadly if it travels to places like your lungs, inhibiting breathing.

Adverse reactions to medication

You may have an adverse reaction to the medications administered during surgery, resulting in dangerously low blood pressure. You must inform your healthcare team of any drug allergies beforehand. Because there may be no way of knowing who may have an adverse reaction to a given medication, the medical team will monitor your heart, breathing, blood pressure and other vital signs during surgery to prevent or immediately act on any danger signs. You can also do your due diligence by researching these medications before consenting.

Organ or tissue damage

I mentioned above that when removing tumours, surgeons remove some healthy tissue to ensure they get the whole tumour.[61] Unfortunately, that can damage other organs such as the kidneys, lungs, or heart. Issues with these organs are more likely to occur if you have medical problems with them.[62] Some blood vessels can be damaged during your surgery.

Impediment of other bodily functions

After surgery, you might experience energy loss, tiredness or hardship getting out of bed and walking. You may also have issues using the toilet. Further on in this book, there is information about the long-term side effects of specific types of cancer surgeries.

How successful are cancer surgeries?

There are rare cases where cancer can spread during a small needle biopsy. That is more likely for some liver and kidney cancers, but there is still a slight chance with other biopsies. However, improvements in how biopsies are done make this chance almost negligible. Nonetheless, experimental evidence suggests surgery may create an environment conducive to tumour growth.

Models done on animals show that areas of trauma (such as the surgery point) are conducive to tumour growth in the original area and other points within the body. Recent research evidence also suggests that the probability of liver metastasis increases after surgery, causing new local and regional metastatic foci and tumour growth. However, no clinical studies explicitly show such results, so the concept is debatable.[63]

Administering systematic pre-surgery treatments improves the effectiveness of cancer surgeries.

A new option for cancer patients arrived recently through systematic treatments. Systematic treatments are medications that go through the body and treat the cancer wherever they find it. They have resulted in more limited surgeries or, in some cases, the patient needing no surgery at all. This treatment has been particularly helpful in cases where surgery is not an option, such as with "unresectable" tumours that have grown too big and gone deeper into tissues. Systematic therapy shrinks the tumour, which is then surgically removed.

According to the 2020 Clinical Cancer Advances Report, three cancers, melanoma, kidney cancer, and pancreatic cancer, have been successfully treated with systematic therapy.[64] Melanoma is "the deepest layer of the epidermis, just above the dermis".[65]

Treating melanoma

Results from two 2019 studies show that systematic therapy before surgery improves treatment results for those suffering from locally advanced melanoma.

In the first study, two combined targeted therapy drugs, dabrafenib and trametinib, were given to 35 patients before their surgery. The results were that by the time surgery was to take place, 86% of the patients' tumours shrunk, and 46% showed no signs of cancer whatsoever. Afterwards, the U.S. Food and Drug Administration (FDA) approved the combination drug for "treating advanced melanoma with a BRAF V600 mutation".

In the second study, lower doses of two immunotherapies, ipilimumab (yervoy) and nivolumab (opdivo), were used to treat locally advanced melanoma. Image scans showed that tumours shrank in 57% of patients. Even more surprising, when checked using tissue samples, the tumours had shrunk in 77% of patients. Their side effects also decreased when checked after 12 weeks.[66]

Treating kidney cancer

Studies published in 2019 suggest that targeted therapy medications could end the need for kidney surgery.

In the first study of 450 patients, some were treated with sunitinib alone and others with surgery followed by sunitinib. The results showed that those treated with only sunitinib lived a median of 18.4 months, compared to those who had surgery before receiving the medication, who lived a median of 13.9 months.

The second study involved patients with clear cell metastatic renal cell carcinoma. Some were treated with surgery right away. Others had their surgery delayed until after sunitinib treatment. The patients treated first with sunitinib and then surgery lived 17.4 months longer than those treated with surgery right away.

Treating pancreatic cancer

In some cases, surgery is not an option for treating pancreatic cancer, or where surgery is an option, only partial tumour removal is possible. 2019 studies showed that starting treatment with systematic therapies and then surgery had better outcomes.

In both studies, doctors used a combination of chemotherapy and radiotherapy to shrink the tumours and then surgically remove them.

In the first study, a phase II clinical trial involving 48 participants with borderline resectable pancreatic ductal carcinoma, participants were treated with folfirinox. Patients whose cancer no longer affected their blood vessels were given a short course of proton-beam radiation therapy combined with an oral chemotherapy medication named xeloda. They had surgery one to three weeks later. Patients whose cancer was still in the blood vessels were given a longer course of external proton-beam therapy combined with capecitabine or fluorouracil. Surgeons operated four to eight weeks later. Thirty-one of the forty-eight participants were able to have surgery, and 67% had no signs of cancer cells in the location afterwards. The media-progression-free survival rate increased from 15 to 49 months for those who had surgery. After two years, 72% of those who had surgery were still alive, whereas the overall study survival rate was only 56%. Thus, most of the living patients were those who could undergo surgery after the pre-treatments.

In the second study of 49 participants with locally advanced pancreatic cancer, doctors used losartan with folfirinox and radiation therapy. Patients whose tumours could be removed were given a short course of proton-beam radiation and capecitabine. Those with cancer in their blood vessels were given a long course of external-beam radiation therapy along with fluorouracil or capecitabine. The treatment resulted in 61% of patients having no cancer cells in the area where the tumour had been. The median progression-free survival after surgery increased from 17.5 to 21.3 months. The median overall survival rose from 31.4 to 33 months for those who had surgery.[67]

Hormone and Targeted Therapies are sophisticated and target specific genes and proteins that feed cancer growth. For example, oestrogen fuels breast cancer. To treat breast cancer, doctors use medications such as Tamoxifen that block the hormone's effects.

The journey after a cancer diagnosis is undeniably challenging. Therefore, understanding the treatment options reduces stress and makes the path less daunting.

Changing Your Lifestyle to Enhance Your Cancer Treatment

I have outlined the various medical interventions available for treating cancer. While those treatments have proved effective, they are ineffective on their own because medical treatment only targets the disease's physiological aspect.

However, the broader canvas of cancer treatment encompassing emotional, psychological, and overall lifestyle factors is often not addressed. Many research projects have revealed that a truly comprehensive approach to cancer intervention integrates traditional medical treatments with holistic lifestyle changes. These changes include diet, physical activities, and holistic and alternative therapies. The following section explores the essential facets of these lifestyle changes, focusing on dietary adaptations, physical activity, and the realm of holistic and alternative therapies.

Dietary Changes to Support Treatment and Recovery

Hippocrates once said, "Let food be thy medicine, and let medicine be thy food."

> The adage *you are what you eat* rings true, especially when you are diagnosed with cancer. Dietary choices support medical treatments, aiding recovery and fortifying the body against potential relapses.

Eat a Nutritionally Rich Diet

Nutrient-rich foods such as organic vegetables, whole grains, and lean proteins ensure the body gets essential vitamins and minerals. Such diets support cellular repair and bolster the immune system.[68]

Stay Hydrated

Drinking adequate water is essential for detoxing the body and alleviating some side effects of chemotherapy, such as constipation and fatigue.[69]

Limit Processed Foods

If possible, remove processed foods from your diet altogether. If circumstances do not permit, reducing your processed food intake reduces inflammation and supports overall health.[70]

Manage Your Dietary Side Effects

Cancer treatments sometimes lead to loss of appetite, taste changes, or digestive issues. You need food to maintain your strength. Therefore, to strike the balance between your need for food and loss of appetite, you must tailor your diet to fit the circumstances. You might opt for softer foods and smaller, more frequent meals.[71]

Why Physical Activity Matters

Movement and exercise may appear counterintuitive during illness when you are obviously weak. However, they significantly enhance the quality of your life and cancer treatment outcomes. Engaging in physical activity tailored to your capacity significantly improves your stamina, reduces treatment side effects, and elevates your mood. The role of physical activity in cancer treatment is to strengthen your frame.

Exercise Boosts Physical Well-being

Regular, moderate exercise reduces fatigue, improves cardiovascular health, and increases muscle strength. These improve post-surgery recovery.[72]

Exercise Boosts Mental Health

Physical activity reduces symptoms of depression and anxiety in cancer patients. The endorphin release associated with exercise can elevate mood and overall well-being.[73]

Physical Activity Supports Recovery

Post-treatment exercise aids and speeds healing, improves physical function and reduces the risk of cancer recurrence.[74]

Holistic Therapies: Bridging Mind and Body

Medical interventions address the physical manifestations of cancer. However, after cancer, the mind and spirit also need healing. Holistic therapies, including meditation, yoga and acupuncture, are excellent ways to heal your whole system and help you move on from the emotional and psychological burden of having had cancer.

ACTION PLAN

Step 1

Request detailed information about your cancer type, stage, and other relevant medical details from your doctor.

Step 2

Research or ask your medical team about the specifics of your cancer type. Use reputable sources like the American Cancer Society, National Cancer Institute, or Cancer Research UK for information.

Step 3

Study the various treatment plans, including surgery, chemo, radiation, immunotherapy, targeted and hormone therapies, and clinical trials available for your type of cancer.

Step 4

Schedule a detailed discussion with your oncologist to go over your treatment options. Ask about the goal of each treatment (curative vs. palliative).

Step 5

Review the potential side effects and long-term implications of each treatment option. Ask your healthcare team about strategies for managing the side effects.

Step 6

Consider each treatment's impact on your quality of life, including time commitment, physical impact, and cost.

Step 7

If unsure about the proposed treatment plan, seek a second opinion.

Step 8

Discuss your treatment options with your family and friends. They will be your core support team during treatment.

Step 9

Research integrative therapies such as dietary support, physical therapy, or complementary medicine to complement your treatment.

Step 10

Research the possibility of enrolling in a clinical trial. Some might be suitable for your type of cancer.

Step 11

Weigh the information, advice, and personal considerations to decide on your best treatment option.

Step 12

Work with your healthcare team to schedule your treatments to fit your commitments.

Step 13

Prepare for the treatment both physically and psychologically. That might include organising transportation, meal preparation, and care responsibilities.

Step 14

Keep up to date with new treatments or changes in recommendations as research evolves.

Step 15

Regularly review the effectiveness of your treatment with your oncologist and be prepared to adjust the plan if necessary.

Step 16

Use support services like counselling, financial advice, and patient support groups.

Remember, you should choose your treatment in close consultation with your healthcare team and consider the most up-to-date medical advice and personal preferences.

Chapter Six: How to Manage Your Treatment Side Effects

There is no disguising the fact that cancer treatment can be brutal. I have said in previous chapters that "you have cancer" are the most dreaded words anyone could hear and often provoke shock and apprehension. Most of us know there is a chance we could die from the disease, but the main reason for the dread is the treatment. Almost everyone is aware of the brutality and howling side effects of cancer treatment and the physical, emotional, and psychological impacts it brings. The side effects frequently include nausea, fatigue, pain, changes in appearance, and emotional distress. Effectively managing the side effects is crucial for your comfort and overall well-being.

With several treatments and challenges, the cancer journey is a profound test of resilience. Knowledge, proactive communication, and supportive care help navigate the voyage.

How Treatment Impacts Your Quality of Life

Recognising how the side effects impact your quality of life and developing coping mechanisms are crucial for maintaining physical, emotional, and psychological well-being during your treatment.

The impacts of the side effects include the following:

Physical Discomfort

Sometimes, the side effects cause pain and discomfort and limit daily activities.

Emotional Impact

The side effects can be emotionally draining, leading to anxiety, depression, and stress.

Social and Lifestyle Changes

The side effects can result in changes in appearance, diet, and your ability to engage in physical activities.

Common Cancer Treatment Side Effects

Cancer treatments produce a range of side effects depending on the type of treatment, your health, and your age. While treatments combat cancer, they often come with side effects because they impact healthy cells.

These may include the following:

Surgery Side Effects: pain, fatigue, and temporary changes in body function (for example, bladder function after prostate surgery).[75]

Chemotherapy Side Effects: nausea, vomiting, anaemia, infection, hair loss, fatigue, and changes in blood counts. The side effects depend on the type and amount of the drug(s) administered.[76]

Radiation Therapy Side Effects: skin changes (similar to sunburn), severe fatigue, and localized pain or fibrosis.[77]

Immunotherapy Therapy Side Effects: immune-related problems such as skin rash, diarrhoea, fatigue, flu-like symptoms, a drop in blood pressure and inflamed organs.[78]

Targeted Therapy Side Effects: rashes or other skin problems, high blood pressure, fatigue, and issues related to blood clotting and wound healing.[79]

Communicating with your healthcare providers

This is the most essential and fundamental step. Be open, honest, and as straightforward as possible when talking to your healthcare provider.

Communicate your side effects to your healthcare team promptly, they might offer remedies, adjust your treatment, and provide support.

Maintain Contact with Your Healthcare Team

Do your best to maintain regular appointments and discussions with your healthcare team to monitor and manage your side effects. Be straightforward about your symptoms, their severity, and how they impact you.

Medication for Symptom Management

In some instances, medicines alleviate side effects and help manage the symptoms. These include the following:

Anti-nausea medications: help manage chemotherapy-induced nausea and vomiting.

Pain Management: There are lots of options for managing pain. Discuss them and their benefits with your healthcare team.

Complementary Therapy, such as acupuncture, massage, and yoga, helps ease cancer treatment side effects. Mind-body practices like meditation and mindfulness also help, especially with reducing stress.

Physical Activity and Exercise, even at a reduced intensity, have enormous benefits for reducing side effects. They also reduce your risk of developing diseases, strengthen your bones and muscles, manage your weight, and improve brain function and quality of life.[80]

Studies show that consistent exercise reduces your chances of developing dementia, including Alzheimer's disease, and improves memory and attention.

Exercise reduces anxiety, and depression, improves sleep, reduce the need for medication.

Regular, moderate exercise lowers the chance of developing cancers (in your case, new cancers), including in the breast, bladder, colon, kidney, stomach, and prostate.[81]

Two and the half hours per week (30 minutes per day for five days) is enough to maintain your weight and lower the risk of heart disease and stroke because it lowers your blood pressure and cholesterol, the leading causes of death in the United States.

It also reduces your chances of becoming a type-2 diabetic or having metabolic syndrome/insulin resistance syndrome.[82] Metabolic syndrome increases your risk of coronary heart disease, stroke, diabetes, and other serious health issues.[83] Health conditions that lead to metabolic syndrome include excess fat around your waistline, high blood sugar, high blood pressure, low HDL, and high triglycerides.[84]

You might be surprised to learn that, according to the CDC,[85] regular exercise also makes you 50% less likely to die from the flu, pneumonia or other viruses. That is because, during exercise, the propensity of your immune system to activate inflammatory responses and stress hormones decreases. Better still, the levels of natural killer (NK) cells, immature B cells, lymphocytes and monocytes increase.[86] NK cells are your white blood cells that kill infected cells and cancer cells within your body.[87] B cells attach themselves to pathogens and disable them.[88] Lymphocytes and monocytes also destroy pathogens through different processes.[89]

Exercise gives you the strength to carry out your daily activities by lowering your risk of functional limitations (the inability to do everyday activities such as climbing the stairs and playing with your children or grandchildren.[90]

Please consult your healthcare team before starting your exercise routine and ensure it is safe and appropriate. A physical therapist or certified trainer could also develop a personalised exercise plan for your situation.

Supportive Care

Supportive care services help with palliative care and mental health support, such as counselling and therapy, to reduce your emotional distress.

Recognise Emotional Challenges

Never underestimate the emotional toll of cancer treatment. Recognising and addressing emotional challenges is an essential part of your healing process. You must understand that it is normal to experience a range of emotions, including fear, anxiety, and sadness. To deal with those emotions, lean on your support network, including family, friends, and support groups, and share your feelings and concerns.

Seek Professional Help

In addition to your personal support network, you will also benefit from support from mental health professionals. Therapy and counselling help you develop effective coping mechanisms and reduce emotional distress. Medication is another effective tool for dealing with emotional distress because it helps manage anxiety and depression.

Self-Care Stress Reduction Practices

While help from your support network and professionals is important, ultimately, it comes down to your response. Incorporating self-care stress reduction practices into your daily routine significantly improves your emotional well-being. Mindfulness and relaxation practices such as meditation, deep breathing, and progressive muscle relaxation also help reduce your stress. Engaging in hobbies and other fun activities enables you to relax.

Nutrition and Diet

Diet is crucial for managing side effects and maintaining strength during cancer treatment. A well-balanced diet that includes a variety of fruits, vegetables, lean proteins, and whole grains is also an excellent countermeasure for dealing with the side effects of cancer treatment. In some instances, dietary supplements or specialised nutritional support may be necessary.

Food is our fuel. Without it, we lack energy, our organs are unable to function, and we die. However, like a vehicle, if you fill up with dirty petrol or diesel when you have a petrol car, your engine will malfunction. Similarly, consuming junk food damages your body, causing malfunction and disease. When your immune system is already in a battle with an illness like cancer, eating the best food possible helps you survive.

What does the body need to run like a brand-new engine?

Your body feeds via the blood it transports to your organs. Your blood contains plasma, white blood cells, red blood cells, and platelets.

Your blood performs many functions to keep your body healthy:

1. It transports oxygen and nutrients to the lungs and tissues,
2. It carries cells and antibodies to fight off infections,
3. It carries waste to the kidneys and liver, which then filter and clean the blood,
4. It regulates your body temperature,
5. It clots to prevent too much blood loss.[91]

The food you eat makes and feeds your blood. Good food makes good blood.

The food you eat makes and feeds your blood. Good food makes good blood.

Your Body Needs Fibre, Fat, and Protein

The body needs three essential food groups it does not produce: fibre, protein and fat.

Where can you get fibre?

Fibre is an indigestible carbohydrate that comes in soluble and insoluble forms. Soluble fibres dissolve in water, while insoluble fibres do not.

Soluble fibres help lower glucose and blood cholesterol[92] by slowing the breakdown of starch into glucose.[93] Oats, barley, chia seeds, peas, nuts, citrus fruits, lentils, carrots, apples, blueberries, and psyllium are soluble fibres.[94, 95]

Insoluble fibres help food to move smoothly through your digestive tract.[96] Wheat bran, quinoa, brown rice, couscous, legumes, leafy green vegetables, carrots, potatoes, fruits with edible skins, parsnips, fruits with edible seeds, nuts, seeds, walnuts, corn, rye, barley, almonds are insoluble fibres.[97,98, 99]

A 2013-2018 study of 14,600 US adults led by Derek Miketinas PhD, RD, an assistant professor at Texas Woman's University, found that only 5% of men and 7% of women ate the recommended quantity of 25g/2000 calorie diet for women and 38g/2000 for men.[100]

Refined carbohydrates, a significant part of the Western diet, have very little fibre. The refining process removes over 50% of the vitamin B, 90% of the vitamin E, and almost all the fibre. Fortifying them does not replace the removed phytochemicals.[101] Foods stripped of fibre include white flour, white pasta, white bread, potato chips, pretzels, most breakfast cereals, cookies, cakes, and juices.

Fibre is essential for the body to maintain healthy blood and function well. Your diet must have an adequate amount and variety of fibre.

Key Takeaway

Natural fibre is essential for your diet. Start getting your daily intake of fibre today. Don't worry about the amount; just eat various fibrous foods with healthy protein and fats until you are full.

Where can you find good fats and protein?

Your body needs fats to build energy, keep warm, produce hormones, absorb nutrients, and help your cells function. Your liver makes cholesterol from fat. The brain needs that cholesterol to function.[102]

Your body gets good fats from nuts and seeds, including coconuts, almonds, cashews, peanuts, flax, pear, pumpkin, sesame, sunflower, chia, and olive (a fruit, but the seed produces oil).

The Link between seeds and amino acids

Your body needs 20 amino acids, but nine of them only come from your food. The nine essential amino acids are histidine, isoleucine, leucine, lysine, methionine, phenylalanine, threonine, tryptophan, and valine. Your body needs different combinations of amino acids to make proteins.

Amino acids also do the following:

- assist in breaking down food,
- boost your immune system,

- grow and repair your body tissues,
- provide energy,
- sustain your digestive system,
- build muscles.[103]

Every natural seed has all or some of the nine essential amino acids your body needs. Seeds with all nine essential amino acids are complete proteins. Seeds with some of the nine essential amino acids are incomplete proteins.[104]

Complete protein seeds include quinoa, buckwheat, and hempseed.[105]

Seeds with incomplete proteins include flax, pumpkin, sesame, sunflower, and chia. Combining seeds in your meals is the best way to get all nine essential amino acids.

Key Takeaway

You must incorporate good fat in the form of nuts and seeds to provide all the essential amino acids in your diet.

Your diet does not need to be complicated. Eat various natural healthy foods that provide good fats, proteins and fibre.

To make the change less daunting, below are foods ideas for breakfast and lunch with recipes for a balanced diet.

Healthy breakfast recipes for cancer patients

Breakfast, as the name suggests, should break the fast that occurred through the night hours while you slept. It should be the heaviest meal of the day because the body needs the energy for the day's work.

Include these things in your breakfast and lunch recipe:

- Vegetables or fruits (do not mix the two, if avoidable),
- Whole food that has natural fibre,
- Grains,
- Nuts,

Here is a website with some great, healthy recipe ideas for breakfast, lunch, and a third meal (if taken). You can tweak or combine to satisfy your stomach.

https://rainbowplantlife.com/category/recipes/?fwp_recipes_categories=vegan-breakfast&fwp_recipes_diets=refined-sugar-free

On the website, you will find:

- Healthy lunch recipes for cancer patients

Lunch should be lighter than breakfast and no less than five hours afterwards. Avoid snacks between breakfast and lunch, not even a peanut.

Include the following in your lunch recipe:

- vegetables or fruits (do not mix the two, if avoidable),
- whole foods with natural fibre,
- grains,
- nuts,

- Healthy dessert recipes for cancer patients

Though you can add a third very light meal daily, two meals are better because each must be five hours apart.

- Healthy side dishes for cancer patients

General recommendations from the American Cancer Society

If You Are Suffering From Constipation

- increase your daily intake of high-fibre foods (with your doctor's permission),
- drink plenty fluids (natural juices and water),
- exercise (walking is simple and easy for most of us),
- avoid foods that cause gas: peas, beans, avocados, apples, milk, sodas, cabbage, and broccoli,
- do not chew gum,
- avoid eggs and cheese,
- do not use enemas or suppositories.[106]

If You Are Suffering From Diarrhea

- take a clear liquid diet at the onset of diarrhoea,
- do not drink acidic liquids,
- eat foods high in potassium (potatoes, bananas, apricots),
- consume foods and liquids high in sodium (soups, broths),
- drink one cup of liquid after each bowel movement,

- avoid dairy products, pastries, high-fat foods, alcohol, tobacco, and high-fibre foods.[107]

If You Are Suffering From Chemo Brain

- write down what you wish to remember in a daily planner,
- avoid demanding tasks,
- get plenty of rest and sleep,
- eat lots of vegetables,
- avoid multitasking,
- avoid alcohol.[108]

If You Are Suffering From Mouth Sores and Pain

- eat soft foods,
- use a straw,
- avoid acidic drinks, alcohol and tobacco,
- avoid spicy, salty foods,
- avoid sour fruits like tomatoes, oranges, and limes,
- keep your lips moist,
- drink plenty of water daily.[109]

For a complete list of cancer side effects and possible remedies, visit the American Cancer Society website at:

https://www.cancer.org/cancer/managing-cancer/side-effects.html

Make Use of Rehabilitation Services

Rehabilitation services, including physical and occupational therapy, help you regain physical function and address treatment-related impairments. Physical therapists help with mobility, pain management, and improving physical functions. Occupational therapists focus on helping you perform daily activities and tasks more easily.

Advances in Cancer Treatment Side Effect Management

Medical research continues to advance our understanding of cancer treatment side effects and how to manage them. Some advances include the following:

Targeted Therapies: Advances in targeted therapies have led to treatments with fewer side effects and better outcomes for some cancers.

Precision Medicine: Personalised treatment plans based on genetic and molecular factors effectively reduce treatment side effects.

Patient-Centred Research

Patients and advocacy groups actively participate in research planning, ensuring that side effects management aligns with your priorities and needs. New cancer treatments consider survival rates and factor in the patient's quality of life during and after treatment.

Managing cancer treatment side effects requires knowledge, support, resilience, open, honest communication with healthcare team, comprehensive symptom management, including medication, complementary therapies, supportive care, recognising and addressing emotional challenges, physical rehabilitation, and nutrition.

Resources

Consult Your healthcare team: Seek guidance from your healthcare professionals.

Supportive Services: Explore palliative care and psychological support services.

Patient Advocacy Groups: Organisations like Cancer Research UK and Macmillan Cancer Support offer resources and guidance.

Exercise and Nutrition: Consult a physical therapist or nutritionist for personalized plans.

Clinical Trials: Explore clinical trials that focus on minimising side effects.

ACTION PLAN

Step 1

Seek detailed information from your healthcare team about the potential side effects of your treatments.

Step 2

Before starting treatment, discuss strategies for managing the side effects with your healthcare team.

Step 3

Study the treatments' side effects to enable you plan mitigation strategies in advance. Get anti-nausea or other symptom-relieving medications from your healthcare team.

Step 4

Write down a detailed description of the side affects you experience. Note their severity, duration, and any triggers or alleviating issues.

Step 5

Inform your healthcare team of your side effects as soon as possible. That helps them adjust your treatment.

Step 6

Research how non-medical therapies such as acupuncture can help you manage the side effects.

Step 7

Seek the help of mental health professionals with expertise in cancer treatment side effect coping strategies.

Step 8

Engage in gentle exercise like walking or yoga and rest as much as possible. Exercise improves energy levels and reduces fatigue and side effects.

Step 9

You might experience skin-related side effects, so develop a self-care routine to manage them. Use sensitive skin products.

Step 10

Cancer treatment can result in severe fatigue. Conserve your energy, take short naps, and prioritise your daily tasks.

Step 11

Join local cancer support groups and learn how others cope with their side effects.

Step 12

Cancer treatment side effects can incapacitate you. So, seek assistance to manage the financial and employment implications of your side effects.

Step 13

Your family and caregivers need to be aware of the side effects of your treatment, including how they impact your interactions with them and how they can support you in managing them.

Step 14

Your healthcare team will regularly assess the impact of your side effects, adjust your treatment and give you management strategies.

Step 15

You might have long-term side effects. Ask your healthcare team and support network for help in developing strategies for coping with them.

Chapter Seven: Non-Medical Treatment Might Work for You

Cancer treatments like surgery, chemo, and radiation therapy have advanced significantly. While they have saved countless lives, they often have severe side effects, including nausea, fatigue, and hair loss, and may not always cure you. They can be daunting, often laced with uncertainty and challenging decisions. Non-medical interventions could make the process more palatable.

> Let me insert a word of caution into this section. Cancer is a deeply personal journey often fraught with uncertainty and fear. Many patients navigate the journey through conventional medicine. However, there are an increasing number of cancer patients drawn to non-medical interventions. This book is primarily about traditional medicine. However, I include some information about non-medical treatments in case some readers, including you, are inclined to seek the non-medical intervention paths.

You must carefully think through your decision to integrate non-medical intervention into your cancer treatment after thorough research and expert guidance tailored to your unique medical and personal circumstances. Ensure you evaluate the potential interactions with modern medical therapies and seek documented evidence of efficacy and safety. Furthermore, you must make your decision to use non-medical treatments in collaboration with your healthcare provider.

Even though non-medical interventions combine well with medical interventions ease the suffering of cancer patients, some medical professionals scorn the idea. That is because some unscrupulous individuals tout non-medical intervention as a replacement for medical intervention. However, that is mostly in cases where traditional medicine can no longer cure or provide relief.

While it is true that non-medical interventions sometimes shrink cancer tumours, those cases are few and far between. Non-medical interventions can never replace proper medical interventions. However, when used together, they can work well

While it is true that non-medical interventions sometimes shrink cancer tumours, those cases are few and far between. Non-medical interventions can never replace proper medical interventions. However, when used together, they can work well.

Non-medical intervention represents a spectrum of practices that fall outside modern medicine. Some focus on the physical aspects, while others aim to balance the emotional and spiritual well-being of the patient.

These therapies range from ancient practices rooted in traditional medicine to contemporary therapies based on recent scientific findings.

Unlike conventional treatments, including surgery, chemo, and radiation therapy, non-medical interventions are rarely backed by clinical trials. They may be inspired by cultural traditions, personal beliefs, or holistic philosophies prioritising natural and non-invasive healing methods.

Most focus on the holistic health paradigm, which views healing as integrating mind, body, and spirit rather than eradicating disease. They integrate biological, nutritional, psychological, and physical principles.

Non-medical intervention includes dietary changes, mind-body techniques like yoga and meditation, herbal remedies, and lifestyle modifications. Their role in cancer treatment complements medical intervention by addressing the process' physical, emotional, and psychological aspects. Importantly, they help manage side effects.

The most common non-medical therapies

Herbal Remedies use plants that fight cancer directly or alleviate symptoms. They include herbal teas and supplements that have been used for centuries to manage cancer.

Many people combine vitamins, minerals and herbs with conventional medicinal treatments. The National Center for Complementary and Alternative Medicine (NCCAM) has revealed that many cancer patients are using these methods as part of their cancer treatment plan.[110]

According to one study, 91% of cancer patients combine non-conventional and conventional cancer therapies.[111] Others use herbs to alleviate the numerous side effects that result from contemporary cancer treatment. Ginger, flax seed, and ginseng have been clinically tested and proven effective in alleviating cancer symptoms and symptoms resulting from conventional cancer interventions.

Other examples include turmeric, which has anti-inflammatory properties, mistletoe extract, which some studies suggest may boost the immune system; and green tea extracts, which contain polyphenols that some laboratory studies suggest may have anti-cancer effects. Essiac, a blend of herbs including burdock root and sheep sorrel, is traditionally believed to detoxify the body and boost the immune system. Some believe that milk thistle protects liver cells during chemotherapy.

It's important you consult with your healthcare providers before incorporating herbs into your regimen because some of them may interact with your pharmaceutical medications.

Acupuncture is an ancient Chinese practice involving inserting fine needles into specific points of the body. It is believed to rebalance the body's energy, or qi, and many people use it for pain relief, stress management and chemotherapy-induced nausea.

Dietary Changes: Diet plays a crucial role in cancer prevention and management. Certain foods and nutrients have protective effects. For example, a diet rich in fruits and vegetables provides essential vitamins and antioxidants that bolster the immune system and reduce cancer risk.

Many diets focus on strengthening the immune system. Various healthy diets, from plant-based to specific "superfoods" possess anti-cancer properties. Ketogenic or macrobiotic diets limit the growth of cancer cells. Berries and nuts rich in antioxidants also have anti-cancer properties.

Understanding Differences in Non-Medical Therapies

There are few differences between alternative, complementary, and integrative therapies. You must understand the distinctions before choosing the best for you.

Alternative Therapies: Some people use alternative therapies unsupported by evidence from rigorous clinical trials in place of conventional treatments. You should be cautious when using alternative therapies as they could interfere with your conventional medicine.

Complementary Therapies used alongside standard treatments may alleviate symptoms, address the psychological and spiritual aspects of cancer care, and improve quality of life. Examples include mind-body therapies and meditation for stress relief or gentle exercise, including yoga for physical strength and flexibility.

Integrative Therapies are a holistic approach that blends conventional and complementary treatments. It is a coordinated way to support your overall health and well-being during and after traditional cancer treatment. Integrative oncology centres often include a team of oncologists, nutritionists, psychologists, and alternative therapy practitioners.

Research indicates that a significant percentage of cancer patients use non-medical interventions alongside medical treatments. According to several studies and meta-analyses, the percentage of cancer patients in the United States incorporating complementary therapy into their cancer care plan ranged from 22% to 91%.[112]

The Steps for Seeking Non-Medical Interventions

If you want to use non-medical interventions as part of your cancer treatment, adequate information is essential.

Us the following steps as a guide:

Consult Your Healthcare Team: Discuss your intention to incorporate non-medical interventions with your primary healthcare team. They can provide guidance and ensure they align with your medical treatment.

Research Thoroughly: Research and understand the specific non-medical interventions you are interested in. Use reputable sources such as peer-reviewed journals and websites.

Seek Professional Guidance: Consult specialists in non-medical interventions.

Dr Jeremy R. Geffen, president of Geffen Visions International, Inc., and director of integrative oncology of P4 Healthcare and Caring4Cancer.com, states that some herbs "lower the toxicity of chemotherapy drugs". However, he cautions that the same herbs may also lower the drug's effectiveness and increase its toxicity, making the patient feel even worse.[113]

In deciding on herb and conventional cancer treatment combinations, it is best to avoid trying out any and every concoction highlighted in online blogs. I encourage you to:

a. Contact a naturopathic oncologist experienced in dealing with your cancer type who is knowledgeable about the best herbs to use. They can observe and test to determine if any combination works or hinders your recovery. Try the Oncology Association of Naturopathic Physicians (ONCANP), which has over 400 naturopathic physicians and students. 115 of them are certified fellows of the American Board of Naturopathic Oncologists.[114] Visit https://www.oncanp.org/find-an-nd#!directory/map and find a naturopathic oncologist to help.

b. Seek CAM clinical trials from the National Cancer Institute at http://www.cancer.gov/clinicaltrials/search

Integrate Carefully: Don't go cold turkey; incorporate non-medical interventions carefully. Please pay careful attention to how your body reacts to them, then slowly make changes while informing your medical team of what you are doing.

Monitor and Adjust: Regularly assess the impact of non-medical interventions on your health. Make adjustments and proceed cautiously.

Join Supportive Communities: Join cancer support groups or communities that focus on non-medical interventions. They can provide valuable insights and emotional support.

The Science of Non-Medical Intervention

Non-medical interventions have been the subject of a growing body of research testing their efficacy. The studies vary in methodology, sample size, and rigour and are preliminary, often conducted in vitro (in the laboratory) or in vivo (in animals), which may not translate to human benefit. The evidence varies in quality.

Another area of active research is mind-body practices, such as meditation and yoga for cancer. Clinical trials show they significantly reduce anxiety and depression, improve quality of life, and impact biological markers of stress and inflammation.

For example, several studies on high-dose vitamins like vitamin C suggest they increase the efficacy of chemotherapy. However, other studies show no significant benefits. Phytochemicals, active compounds found in plants, have also been studied extensively. Resveratrol found in grapes and sulforaphane from cruciferous vegetables has demonstrated anti-cancer properties. Medicinal mushrooms like Reishi and Turkey Tail have potential immune-modulating and anti-tumour effects. However, translating these findings to human treatment is complex, and effective doses and long-term effects remain unclear. Mind-body practices have perhaps the most supportive evidence among alternative therapies. Numerous studies indicate that mindfulness meditation, tai chi, and yoga significantly reduce stress and improve the quality of life for cancer patients.

However, research into non-medical interventions is limited. Many have not had the same rigorous testing as medical treatments. There are often gaps in the data regarding long-term outcomes, optimal dosing, and potential interactions with standard therapies. One major limitation is the lack of large-scale, random controlled trials, the gold standard for evaluating treatment efficacy. Without these trials, we cannot know if the observed benefits are due to the treatment itself or other factors. Additionally, we must consider the placebo effect as believing their efficacy could influence patient-reported outcomes.

Comparative analysis between non-medical intervention and conventional medical treatments is complex. Conventional treatments work for the majority. Chemotherapy, for example, has a quantifiable success rate regarding tumour reduction and survival rates. Conversely, non-medical intervention lacks such data. However, in some cases, non-medical interventions synergise with conventional treatments. For example, acupuncture helps manage nausea and vomiting associated with chemotherapy.

The following are key findings:

A meta-analysis published in the Journal of the National Cancer Institute (2020) found that mind-body interventions, including meditation and yoga, can improve cancer-related symptoms such as pain and fatigue.[115]

Dietary modifications, such as adopting a plant-based diet, are associated with a reduced risk of certain types of cancer and improved treatment outcomes.[116]

Herbal remedies like ginger and turmeric have demonstrated anti-inflammatory and anti-cancer properties in pre-clinical studies.[117]

These findings underscore the potential benefits of non-medical interventions integrated with medical treatment. However, do your homework. Study any approach you decide on carefully and consult your healthcare provider.

Making informed decisions about non-medical therapy is complex and requires careful thought and consulting your healthcare team. Weigh your options and recognise the importance of evidence-based practices.

Consider The Following:

Your State of Health: Before considering non-medical therapy, ensure you have a full health check, including laboratory tests, scans, and a review of your medical history. Your current state of health, including energy levels, nutritional status, physical fitness, immune system function and comorbidities, impacts non-medical therapy's appropriateness and timing.

Your Cancer Specifics: You must consider the type, stage, and rate of progression of your cancer when deciding on non-medical intervention. Bear in mind the molecular and genetic profile of cancer influences its response to treatment. The progression of cancer is a significant factor. An experimental approach with non-medical therapy may not be so alarming in early-stage cancers. However, the same approach with advanced-stage cancer might be a hazardous proposition.

Existing Medical Conditions: Chronic conditions such as diabetes or heart disease influence the body's response to treatment. For example, diabetes slows or prevents wounds from healing.

Current or Previous Medications: Some non-medical therapies interact with prescription medications, causing adverse effects and reducing treatment efficacy. Previous treatments may also influence the body's ability to respond to new therapies positively. Therefore, if you decide to use non-medical therapy, consider the possible impacts of both past and present treatments.

Enrol Your Healthcare Providers: You must enrol your healthcare team for help in choosing non-medical therapy. They will guide you through decision-making because they have expertise, knowledge, and access to the latest research.[118]

Points to Remember:

Please remember the following points when deciding on non-conventional cancer treatment:

- Non-medical interventions can complement your medical treatments.
- Consult your healthcare team before incorporating non-medical approaches.
- Thoroughly research before choosing a non-medical intervention and ensure it aligns with your requirements.
- Monitor the treatment's impact and be open to adjustments.
- Engage with supportive communities and seek guidance from professionals.

Some Final Thoughts

Make your decision to pursue non-medical therapy when you have a clear understanding of your cancer treatment. When integrated at the appropriate time, it can effectively relieve symptoms.

Pre-Treatment

Before starting conventional treatment, assess non-medical therapies that could reduce the side effects or improve your quality of life.

Now is the best time for preventive measures such as dietary changes and stress reduction therapies.

Mid-Treatment

During your cancer treatment, non-medical therapies can alleviate the side effects and help with the physiological and psychological stress.

Post-Treatment

Non-medical therapies can support recovery and long-term wellness after primary treatment. Physical therapies such as yoga improve physical function. Meditation helps psychological health.

ACTION PLAN

The following is a step-by-step action plan for considering non-medical therapy:

Step 1

Obtain details about your specific type of cancer, the stage, and prognosis from your oncologist.

Step 2

List the symptoms or side effects you wish to manage with non-medical therapy.

Step 3

Research non-medical therapies for your type of cancer, focusing on evidence-based results.

Step 4

Share your findings with your oncologist and ask for their input.

Step 5

Consult an integrative medicine specialist.

Step 6

Research information from reputable cancer organisations, peer-reviewed journals, and government health resources.

Step 7

Avoid sources that promise cures or lack scientific backing.

Step 8

Weigh the potential benefits of the non-medical therapies against any risks or side effects.

Step 9

Consider how these therapies might interact with your conventional treatment plan and consult your medical team.

Step 10

Investigate the costs of your non-medical therapy and explore the possibility of insurance coverage.

Step 11

Research patient assistance programs that might subsidise non-medical therapies.

Step 12

Based on your research and consultations, decide which non-medical therapy you want to pursue.

Step 13

Ensure that your decision is informed, aligns with your values, and is made in collaboration with your healthcare provider.

Step 14

Keep a detailed journal of your non-medical treatment, noting how you feel and any changes in your symptoms.

Step 15

Regularly share that information with your medical team.

Step 16

Adapt your treatment plan based on your body's response and emerging information.

Step 17

Stay flexible and open to changes in your treatment.

Remember, your non-medical therapy plan must fit your specific health needs. Approach the process with care, ensuring you take each step with the support and guidance of your medical team.

____

____

____

____

____

____

____

____

Helpful Resources:

The National Center for Complementary and Alternative Medicine (NCCAM)

The Oncology Association of Naturopathic Physicians (ONCANP)

https://www.oncanp.org/find-an-nd#!directory/map

"Can Complementary Therapies Ease Cancer Treatment Symptoms? What the Science Says"

https://time.com/6171230/complementary-integrative-therapies-cancer/

Survey: "Most Cancer Patients Use Complementary or Alternative Medicine"

https://www.cancertherapyadvisor.com/home/cancer-topics/general-oncology/survey-most-cancer-patients-use-complementary-or-alternative-medicine/

Complementary and Alternative Medicine Website: https://www.betterhelp.com/advice/therapy/what-are-cam-therapies/

Chapter Eight: When All Else Fails, How to Take Part in a Clinical Trial

In cancer country, there are times when, no matter what remedy you try, it will fail. Neither medical interventions nor non-medical intervention will work. That is especially true when cancer has spread to other parts of the body. In that case, you might consider participating in a clinical trial. Clinical trials are not a perfect solution because the medication might not be thoroughly tested. However, when you are in a situation where all else has failed, this last throw of the dice might be your only option.

Cancer stages one to three have a high probability of responding to treatment. However, it becomes a Hail Mary situation once it reaches stage four. As mentioned above, cancer treatment has made Olympic advancements. We are almost there. However, there are situations where cancer has overwhelmed the body, making any attempt at intervention impossible. In those circumstances, a clinical trial is your last card.

Oncology has progressed significantly through clinical trials that test new therapies and treatments. These trials offer hope not only for patients but also for future generations.

Participating in a clinical trial might save your life. In addition, you could make an invaluable contribution to developing innovative cancer treatments.

What Are Clinical Trials?

Clinical trials are at the forefront of medical research and innovation. They are systematic investigations that evaluate the safety, efficacy, and potential side effects of new treatments, therapies, and medical interventions. We cannot overstate the importance of clinical trials in oncology; they are the cornerstone of progress.

Clinical trials help researchers to do the following:

Assess New Therapies: Clinical trials evaluate new treatments, drugs, surgical procedures, and medical devices to improve outcomes, reduce side effects, or even cure patients.

Enhance Current Treatments: Trials also explore modifications to existing treatments to enhance their effectiveness or reduce their toxicity.

Study Prevention and Screening: Some clinical trials focus on cancer prevention, early detection, and screening to identify cancer at the earliest, most treatable stage.

Types of Clinical Trials

Clinical trials have different phases, each with different objectives and procedures:

Phase One clinical trials are the first step in testing new treatments on humans. They assess the treatment's safety and dosage. Researchers select a small group of participants and closely monitor them for adverse effects.

Phase Two clinical trials have a larger participant pool. Researchers collect data on a treatment's effectiveness and monitor side effects. Promising treatments move on to stage three.

Phase Three trials have a more extensive and diverse group of participants. These trials compare the new treatment with existing standard therapies. If successful, it may receive regulatory approval.

Phase Four trials occur after regulatory approval and test safety and effectiveness to identify any rare or long-term side effects.[119]

You must understand the purpose of each phase to help you manage expectations and make informed decisions about which stage you might want to participate in.

The Pros and Cons of Clinical Trials

Clinical trials have potential benefits and risks. You must weigh one against the other when considering enrolling.

Potential Benefits:

Access to Cutting-edge Treatments: Clinical trials provide treatments not yet available to the general public. These treatments are often the latest breakthroughs in cancer care.

Expert Medical Care: Researchers and doctors experienced in the specific condition monitor participants closely.

Contributing to Science: By participating, you actively contribute to medical research, leading to better treatments for others in the future.

Potential Risks:

Uncertain Outcomes: Clinical trials are research endeavours; there is no guarantee they work.

Side effects: As with any medical intervention, there may be side effects or adverse reactions that the researchers disclose before you consent.

Time and Commitment: Clinical trials take time and include frequent medical visits, tests, and procedures.

Before signing up, you must have open and honest discussions with your medical team and the trial investigators about the potential benefits and risks.[120]

A Guide to Participating in Clinical Trials

Before participating in a clinical trial, you must research and gather the essential information. The following is a list to guide you through your decision:

Gather Information:

Start by seeking information about your specific diagnosis and the treatments available. That will give you a baseline understanding of the potential benefits of a clinical trial.

Discuss your options with your medical team. They will provide insights into your diagnosis and suggest appropriate clinical trials.

Use reputable information sources like the National Cancer Institute (NCI), American Cancer Society (ACS), and academic medical institutions.

UK residents can visit the Cancer Research UK website https://www.cancerresearchuk.org/about-cancer/find-a-clinical-trial to find clinical trials in which they could participate.

Ask Questions:

Ask about the clinical trial's phase, objectives, treatment and potential side effects.

Inquire about the trial's eligibility criteria to determine if you meet the requirements for enrolment.

Consult with Experts:

Consult the researchers conducting the trial for specific information about the trial's objective, design, procedures, and expectations.

Discuss the matter with your family, friends, and support network. Their input and emotional support are invaluable.

Seek a second opinion from another oncologist or specialist. A fresh perspective will help you make your decision.

Ensure you write down the questions and the answers you receive to organise your thoughts and compare your options.

Keep Your Healthcare Team Informed

Your healthcare team must be heavily involved in your clinical trial decision-making process.

Here's how to effectively engage with them:

Honest Communication:

Establish open and honest communication and share your concerns and preferences.

Be clear about your treatment goals, whether they prioritise extending life, improving your quality of life, or a cure.

Seek Your Oncologist's Guidance:

Consult your oncologist about trials for your specific cancer type and stage to help you understand the risks and benefits. They will help you decide whether to stick to the standard treatments or if it's worth participating in a clinical trial.

HOW TO FIND CLINICAL TRIALS

We have now established the importance of clinical trials in your cancer journey and the decision-making process. The next stage is finding trials that align with your diagnosis and goals.

The following are some practical steps for finding clinical trials:

United States:

The National Cancer Institute at http://www.cancer.gov/clinicaltrials/search is an official US government website where you can locate clinical trials.

ClinicalTrials.gov is a comprehensive database of clinical trials in the United States. You can search for trials based on cancer type, location, and other criteria (Note: however, the US government does not review and approve the safety of all the studies listed on this site).

Cancer Centres: This is where you find information about clinical trials for reputable cancer centres such as MD Anderson Cancer Center, Mayo Clinic, and Dana-Farber Cancer Institute.

Patient Advocacy Groups: You can find resources and guidance on clinical trials from organisations such as the American Cancer Society, and the National Comprehensive Cancer Network (NCCN).

UK:

Cancer Research UK's official website https://www.cancerresearchuk.org/about-cancer/find-a-clinical-trial provides information on ongoing clinical trials, eligibility criteria, and how to enrol.

The National Institute for Health Research (NIHR): NIHR is a valuable resource for finding clinical trials and research studies in the UK.

Use Cancer Centres and Institutions: Search the websites of renowned cancer centres and research institutions.

Use Patient Advocacy Groups: Many patient advocacy organisations, such as the American Cancer Society (ACS) and Cancer Research UK, provide resources to find suitable clinical trials.

Ask Your Doctor and Oncologist: They may have information on trials that are not widely advertised but could work well in your situation.

Use Clinical Trial Matching Services: Some organisations offer clinical trial matching services that use your medical information to identify trials suitable for you.

Explore Local Resources, including university hospitals, medical centres, and community clinics.

Collaborate With Your Healthcare Team in the Following Manner:

Discuss Clinical Trial Options that align with your diagnosis and treatment goals.

Review Eligibility Criteria, including your cancer stage, previous treatments, and overall health.

Ask Your Doctors for Recommendations based on their expertise and knowledge of ongoing clinical trials.

Explore Multiple Clinical Trial Options and discuss them with your healthcare team.

Keep Your Doctors Regularly Updated: Information about your condition or treatment could impact your eligibility for specific trials.

How to Enrol in a Clinical Trial

After identifying and deciding on a clinical trial, you must enrol in it. The following is how to go about the process:

Check the Eligibility Criteria

Every clinical trial has specific eligibility criteria to ensure participant safety and the research result's validity, including the following:

Cancer Type and Stage: Ensure your diagnosis matches the trial's focus.

Previous Treatments: Some trials exclude those who have already undergone specific treatments.

Age and Health are essential criteria for some trials. Therefore, there may be age restrictions or health requirements.

Medical History: Your eligibility for some trials depends on your medical history, including existing health conditions and medication.

Trial Location: Some trials are location-specific, requiring participants to live nearby.

You should carefully review the eligibility criteria to ensure you meet the requirements. If you are unsure, discuss the situation with your healthcare team and the trial investigators.

Informed Consent

Informed consent is essential when you participate in a clinical trial. Informed consent involves a detailed discussion between you and the trial team about the trial's objectives, procedures, risks, and benefits.

The following are some things to expect during the discussion:

Explanation of the Trial: The team will explain the trial's purpose and timeline.

Potential Risks and Benefits: The team already have a clear idea of most of the trial's risks and benefits. Ensure you discuss them until you understand them.

Confidentiality: The team will tell you how they will use your data and medical records to ensure your privacy.

Voluntary Participation: Your participation in any trial is entirely voluntary, so you can stop and withdraw at any time without repercussions. Whatever decision you make will not affect the standard of care you receive.

Questions and Clarifications: Before and throughout the trial, the team will encourage you to ask questions. It's their job to ensure you are well-informed and comfortable with your decision.

Written Consent: The trial team needs your written consent before you can take part. Your written consent shows you understand the trial and are willing to participate.

Before deciding to participate in a clinical trial, take your time. Review the information and ask questions. Seek advice from your medical team, family and support network. The informed consent process protects your rights and ensures your decision is informed and voluntary.[121]

Understanding Trial Phases and Procedures

Clinical trials involve different phases. The following is an outline of what to expect:

Screening: Before beginning the trial, the trial team will screen you to ensure you meet the eligibility criteria. That will probably involve blood tests, imaging scans, and medical assessments.

Eligible: If, after the screening process, you are deemed suitable and selected to participate, you will be administered the treatment according to the trial's protocol, including medications, therapies, and medical procedures.

Monitoring: The trial team will monitor you closely throughout the trial, including regular check-ups, tests, and assessments to track your progress and handle reactions or side effects.

Follow-up: After the trial, there will be a follow-up period when the team continues to monitor you to assess the treatment's long-term effects and outcomes.

Data Collection: Clinical trials collect meticulous data to evaluate the treatment's effectiveness. Your participation helps that process.

Maintain Open Communication: You must maintain open communication with the trial team and report any side effects, concerns, or changes in your health. If you don't, they will be unaware of the trial's impact on your health.[122]

Understanding the phases and procedures lets you prepare and engage in your treatment journey. Always remember that the trial team can answer your questions and concerns even after the trial ends.

Your Clinical Trial Rights

A fundamental ethical principle is protecting your rights when participating in clinical trials. This section explains your rights and the regulatory oversight that safeguards you.

Patient Rights

You are entitled to treatment following specific regulations. Those rights include the following:

Informed Consent: The clinical trial team must provide you with adequate information to make an informed decision about your participation, including the trial's purpose, procedures, risks and benefits. You cannot be penalised for demanding information.

Your Right to Privacy and Confidentiality: To safeguard your privacy, the trial team must keep your personal information and medical records confidential.

Your Right to Medical Care: The clinical trial team must provide you with high-quality medical care by experienced doctors and technicians throughout the trial.

Your Right to Protection from Harm: The clinical trial team must ensure the trial is designed to minimise your risk.

Your Right to Alternative Treatment: The clinical trial team must provide you with information about alternative treatments and therapies, including those outside of the trial.

Your Right to Withdraw: You have the right to withdraw from the trial at any time without consequences, and your decision will not affect your standard of care.[123]

You must be aware of your rights when participating in a clinical trial and assert those rights if necessary. If you ever feel that your rights are not being respected or have concerns about your participation, communicate openly with the team and, if necessary, governmental oversight bodies. In the US, that body is the Institutional Review Board (IRB). In the UK, it is the Medicines and Healthcare Products Regulatory Agency (MHRA).

The Latest Research and Insights on Clinical Trials

There have been numerous advancements in cancer research and treatment. Some notable developments include the following:

Immunotherapy is a cancer treatment game-changer. They harness the body's immune system to target cancer cells. The results are remarkable, leading to long-term remissions and improved survival rates.

Precision Medicine Treatments are tailored to an individual's genetic makeup and their specific cancer characteristics, providing personalised and effective therapies.

Targeted Therapies focus on specific molecules or pathways in cancer growth, resulting in more effective treatments with fewer side effects.

Combination Therapies combine treatments, such as chemotherapy, targeted therapy, and immunotherapy, to enhance effectiveness and overcome resistance.

Advances in early detection and screening have resulted in detecting cancer at its earliest and most treatable stage.

ACTION PLAN

Step 1

Research what clinical trials are available and assess their risks and benefits.

Step 2

Let your healthcare team and specialist know you are interested in participating in a clinical trial and ask for their opinion and recommendations.

Step 3

Research clinical trials for your cancer type using resources such as ClinicalTrials.gov, cancer research centres, and non-profit organisations.

Step 4

Check if you are eligible for the trial by reviewing the eligibility criteria.

Step 5

Consider the logistics of your involvement in the trial, including the location and treatment schedule.

Step 6

Contact the coordinators of the clinical trial you are interested in to request additional information and express your willingness to participate.

Step 7

Carefully review the informed consent form, which outlines all aspects of the trial, including the treatment plan, tests, outcomes, and risks.

Step 8

Seek a second opinion from a different doctor and accurately weigh the trial's pros and cons.

Step 9

Discuss the advantages and disadvantages of participating in the trial with your family and support network.

Step 10

Ask questions you may have about how the trial benefits you.

Step 11

Research insurance coverage and investigate any additional costs of participating in the trial.

Step 12

Communicate your decision about participating in the trial to your healthcare team.

Step 13

Complete the pre-screening tests to confirm your eligibility for the trial.

Step 14

Submit the written informed consent form.

Step 15

When you have enrolled in the trial, ensure you follow the trial protocols and schedules.

Step 16

Monitor your health for any changes and report them to the trial team immediately.

Step 17

Stay up to date about the trial progress for any new information that may affect your participation.

Step 18

Discuss post-trial follow-ups with the trial team to ensure you adhere to them.

Chapter Nine: Coping With Work, Finance, & Relationships During Treatment

Being diagnosed with cancer takes a mental, physical and emotional toll. But there might also be some potential financial challenges that include medical bills, medication, and treatment-related expenses. Beyond the immediate costs, there are possible long-term economic consequences, including your ability to work, ongoing treatments and long-term goals such as mortgages and retirement.

Avoid adding financial stress to your already challenging situation by investigating resources such as insurance and state benefits and take practical steps to ease the burden.

Assess the Possible Impact on Your Work

A cancer diagnosis might change your employment possibilities. Perhaps you will have to take medical leave or adjust your work schedule. As a cancer patient, you must have a strategy including understanding your employment rights, negotiating sick leave and exploring disability benefits.

The extent of the impact on your employment depends on the type and stage of your cancer, your treatment plan, and the terms of your employment. The following list details how your cancer treatment could affect your work.

Can You Continue Working?

Some cancer patients can continue working during their treatment, especially if their cancer is at an early stage and the treatment does not cause severe side effects. Others may not be that lucky. They may require time off work for treatment and recovery. Whatever happens, you must communicate with your employer (or employees). Explain your appointments and treatment, possible downtime and discuss the options.

The Medical Leave Act

The Family and Medical Leave Act (FMLA) in the United States provides most workers with job-protected leave for up to 12 weeks per year for severe health conditions, including cancer. You may qualify for additional medical leave beyond the legal mandate, depending on the terms of your employment contract. Check with your boss or human resources department.

Reasonable Disability Accommodations

Employers are legally obliged to help employees with disabilities, including cancer-related challenges. That includes modifying the workplace, implementing flexible work hours, or implementing a temporary role change.

You could qualify for short or long-term disability insurance benefits during your treatment. Please ensure you investigate that.

Temporary Leave or Disability Insurance

You could qualify for short or long-term disability

insurance benefits during your treatment. Please ensure you investigate that.

Job Loss

You may lose your job due to poor performance caused by the stress of your diagnosis, treatment side effects or employer discrimination. There are laws, such as the Americans with Disabilities Act (ADA), to protect you. If your employer fails to consider your rights, point them out or take legal action. In the UK, you can get legal advice from Citizens Advice.

Learn about your rights under the Family and Medical Leave Act (FMLA). "The FMLA entitles eligible employees of covered employers to take unpaid, job-protected leave for specified family and medical reasons with continuation of group health insurance coverage under the same terms and conditions as if the employee had not taken leave."[124] Contact the FMLA and then discuss the options with your employer. The website for the FMLA is: https://www.dol.gov/agencies/whd/fmla

If you are a UK resident living in England, Scotland, or Wales, you are protected by The Equality Act 2010. You are entitled to reasonable time off for hospital appointments. Whether that is paid or unpaid depends on your employment contract. You are also entitled to statutory sick pay if you are unable to work because of your cancer. As per your contract, you could also claim company sick pay.

You can contact a welfare rights adviser for more information by phoning the Macmillan Support Line free on 0808 808 00 00 from 9 am to 5 pm.[125]

If you are a UK resident living in Northern Ireland, the Disability Discrimination Act 1995 protects you from employer discrimination. You can view the details by clicking the link:

https://www.nidirect.gov.uk/information-and-services/people-disabilities/employment-support-people-disabilities-or-health

Self-employed and Small Business Owners may face unique challenges because they don't have access to the same protections and benefits as employees. However, there are other benefits you may be entitled to. Seek advice from social workers, patient advocacy groups, and legal experts (including the Citizens Advice Bureau in the UK).

Workers' Rights in the UK

Protection from Discrimination:

Like all developed countries, employees in the UK have certain rights to protect and benefit them when diagnosed with cancer.

The following are some of them:

The Equality Act 2010 prohibits discrimination against individuals with cancer or any other disability. Employers cannot treat employees less favourably due to their diagnosis or related treatment.

Reasonable Adjustments

By law, employers must make reasonable adjustments to accommodate cancer patients, including working hours, schedules, responsibilities, environment, and flexible arrangements, such as remote working.

Employees have the right to paid time off for medical appointments related to their cancer diagnosis and treatment. This time off does not count as sick leave.

When ill, employees are entitled to 28 weeks of statutory sick pay (SSP). Some employers offer enhanced sick pay schemes. Ask your boss or human resources department if you are unsure.

Protection Against Unfair Dismissal

The law protects employees diagnosed with cancer against unfair dismissal due to illness or related absences.

Maternity and Paternity Rights

Employees who become parents during their cancer treatment may still be entitled to maternity or paternity leave and benefits.

Retirement Planning

You may be entitled to your pension if you retire or reduce your working hours due to failing health.[126]

How to Cope with Your Finances After a Cancer Diagnosis

Gather and Organise Your Financial Information

A comprehensive financial inventory, including medical bills, insurance policies, income sources, and expenses, is critical to understand your financial situation. Use a dedicated physical or secure electronic folder.

Regularly update the information to make informed decisions, track your expenses, apply for assistance programs, and ensure your financial stability during and after treatment.

Organise the following information:

Income sources: include your salary/wages, rental income, social security, pension, and disability benefits.

Monthly Expenses: Make a detailed list of monthly expenses, including rent or mortgage payments, utilities, groceries, transport, insurance premiums, discretionary spending, credit cards, loans, pension contributions, and subscriptions.

Medical Bills and Expenses: Keep a copy of all medical bills, receipts for co-payments, deductibles, out-of-pocket expenses, prescription costs, health insurance claims and correspondence with your insurance company.

Bank and Investment Account Information: Statements of your checking/current, savings, and investment accounts; stocks, bonds, mutual funds, and outstanding loans, including terms, interest rates, and repayment schedules; and information regarding your creditors and debtor. Include any correspondence from collection agencies.

Support Programs and Financial Assistance: Make and keep a copy of documentation related to any benefits or government assistance programs you qualify for. Also, look for assistance and keep records regarding charitable organisations for cancer patients.

Financial Goals and Planning: List your short and long-term financial goals and priorities.

Legal Documents: Make and keep a copy of important legal documents, such as your will, power of attorney, advance healthcare directives, insurance policies, retirement accounts, trusts and health insurance.

Retirement Accounts: Copy and keep your statements for retirement accounts like 401(k)s, IRAs, or other pension plans, and information regarding your retirement contributions.

Tax Documents: Ensure you keep your previous tax returns, supporting documents, and records of tax deductions related to medical expenses.

Prioritise the Essentials:

First, cover essential expenses such as rent/mortgage, utilities (water, gas and electricity), food, and medical bills.

Cut Unnecessary Expenses:

Identify expenses you can reduce or eliminate, like dining out or non-essential subscriptions. Renegotiate loans or credit card repayments.

Seek Financial Assistance:

Contact organisations like the American Cancer Society, CancerCare, and American Life Fund to solicit financial assistance to help with your medical expenses, transportation, and other expenses you will incur during your cancer treatment.

https://www.cancer.org/

https://www.americanlifefund.com/cancer/financial-assistance/organizations/

UK residents should seek financial support from McMillian Grants and Cancer Research UK to help with energy bills, travelling expenses, and home adaptation plans.

https://www.macmillan.org.uk/cancer-information-and-support/get-help/financial-and-work/macmillan-grants

https://www.cancerresearchuk.org/about-cancer/coping/practically/financial-support

For UK citizens living in Ireland

You can ask for financial support through the Irish Cancer Society and the Comfort Fund.

https://www.cancer.ie/cancer-information-and-support/cancer-support/getting-organised/financial-support

Consider using health savings accounts (HSAs) or flexible spending accounts (FSAs) to pay for qualified medical expenses and save on taxes if you are signed up.

Negotiate Medical Bills

You can negotiate medical bills with your healthcare providers, so negotiate bills and request payment plans. Remember, you will not be offered if you don't ask.

Set Up an Emergency Fund

Create or replenish an emergency fund to cover expenses, including repairs, transportation, or non-covered medical costs.

Consider Long-Term Financial Planning

When you are unwell, focusing on the here and now is typical. Resist that temptation when it comes to money. Assess your long-term finances and adjust to your new circumstances. Consider consulting a financial advisor or counsellor.

Don't Ignore Finance-Related Stress

Do not underestimate the emotional challenge of financial matters when you have cancer. Seek help from your friends, family, or mental health professionals.

Review your financial situation regularly and adjust your budget as needed. Seek help and advice from financial professionals and support organisations while you focus on your health and recovery.

Navigating the Health Insurance Landscape

It can be challenging to deal with health insurance after a cancer diagnosis. However, you must understand and make the most of your insurance coverage. The following is a detailed guide on navigating healthcare insurance after being diagnosed with cancer:

Review Your Insurance Policy

Read through your health insurance policy, paying particular attention to the terms, conditions, and limits. Pay extra attention to the sections concerning cancer treatment, medication, and procedures. Ensure you understand your deductible, co-pays, co-insurance, and out-of-pocket maximum, as these will directly affect your expenses. If you need help, ask family, friends, and your support network, including financial and insurance experts. Ensure you organise all of your insurance-related documents.

In-Network Providers

Use in-network healthcare providers, including doctors, hospitals, and specialists, whenever possible. They are typically covered at a higher rate, so reduce your out-of-pocket costs.

Prior Authorisation

Your insurance company has to authorise some cancer treatments and medication beforehand. Ask your healthcare provider to obtain the necessary approval before commencing treatment.

Understand Benefits and Coverage

Ensure you understand what your insurance policy covers regarding cancer treatments, surgeries, medications, and related services. Ensure you are aware of exclusions and limitations and get confirmation about procedures or visits to specialists.

Maintain Good Records

Keep detailed records of all medical expenses, including bills, receipts, and explanations of benefits (EOBs) provided by your insurer. Your records will be essential for tracking expenses and resolving billing discrepancies.

Clinical Trial Coverage

Some insurance policies cover clinical trial-related expenses, while others may not. You must check your insurance coverage before enrolling in a clinical trial.

Prescription Drug Coverage

Review your health insurance prescription medication coverage. Ensure that your insurance company covers your cancer medications. Ask about preferred or speciality pharmacies that can help reduce the cost.

Coordination of Benefits (COB)

You may have multiple insurance coverage (e.g. through your or your spouse's employer). If that is the case, ensure you understand how they coordinate benefits. You must understand COB rules as they relate to insurance because COB rules determine which insurance is primary and which is secondary.

Appeals and Disputes

If you are denied coverage by your insurance company for a necessary treatment or service, you have the right to appeal against that decision. Your appeal could succeed, especially if the denial relates to treatments that your doctor deems necessary. To ensure you are in a position to win your appeal, you must maintain accurate records of all communication with your insurance company, including dates, times, and the names of those you spoke with.

Seek Clarification

If you are unsure of your insurance policy, ask questions and seek clarification from your insurance company. Whether it is about coverage or billing, talk to your insurance company's customer service or claims department.

Contact Patient Advocates and Social Workers

Most hospitals have a patient advocate group or social workers to help you navigate insurance issues and understand your coverage. Ensure you get in touch with them.

Seek Financial Assistance

Pharmaceutical companies, cancer organisations, and government agencies provide financial assistance programmes to help cover medication and other expenses. Research if you are entitled to any of them.

Consider COBRA and Other Coverage Options

You could lose your job as a result of your illness. You may be eligible for Continuation of Health Coverage (COBRA) or other insurance options if you do. Ensure you are aware of your right to take advantage of them.

Future Coverage

Review your insurance requirements at the end of your cancer treatment and consider updating your coverage based on your health and financial situation.

Navigating health insurance after a cancer diagnosis is challenging. It requires diligence, patience, and advocacy. Familiarise yourself with the terms and conditions, communicate with your healthcare provider, and proactively address any issues to ensure you receive the care you need while managing the costs.

Financial Toxicity

The term financial toxicity describes the economic challenges faced by cancer patients and their families because of the treatment costs.

The following are details about financial toxicity and its impacts:

Direct Costs of Cancer

Cancer treatment is expensive. The initial costs include doctor's visits, hospital stays, lab tests, and imaging scans. Then there is the cost of treatment. Sometimes, even those with health insurance face substantial out-of-pocket expenses, such as deductibles, co-payments, and co-insurance.

Indirect Cancer Expenses

Indirect costs are expenses that are not directly linked to medical treatment but result from having cancer, including transport to and from medical appointments, accommodation near treatment centres, and childcare.

Loss of Income

Loss of income is also an indirect cost of cancer, as patients might be unable to work or engage in economic activities for a long time.

Some may be unable to return to work or need to reduce their working hours because of the physical and emotional toll.

That could result in career stagnation or loss.

Financial Stress and Anxiety

Financial toxicity causes stress and anxiety that can be overwhelming.

Even after recovery, patients without adequate insurance coverage accumulate substantial medical debt, resulting in long-term financial challenges.

Coping Strategies

As a result of financial toxicity, some patients resort to cost-cutting measures, including skipping or rationing medication and delaying or avoiding necessary medical care, which might prove fatal. Furthermore, some might deplete savings or retirement funds or, in extreme cases, file for bankruptcy.

Impact on Quality of Life

Financial toxicity negatively affects anyone's quality of life, resulting in stress, depression, and their willingness or ability to adhere to treatment plans. Addressing the issue and improving your well-being and quality of life is essential.

The following are some ways to mitigate financial toxicity:

Be Aware of your Insurance Coverage: You must understand your health insurance coverage terms and conditions.

To help you do that, seek advice from your insurance company or social worker.

Use Financial Counselling: Most healthcare facilities have financial counsellors available to help patients explore financial assistance programmes, cope with medical bills, and develop payment plans. Ensure you take advantage of them.

Advocacy and Support Groups: For patient assistance programmes offering financial aid, transport, and other resources, talk to patient advocacy and support groups.

Employment and Legal Support: Take advantage of employment assistance programmes, legal advice concerning workplace discrimination and disability help, and access to paid leave or disability benefits.

You must be aware of the impact of financial toxicity and ensure you follow the strategies above to avoid it.

Access to Support Services

Because cancer is physically, emotionally, and financially challenging, support services providing comprehensive care, support and resources are a vital part of the journey.

The following are some support services that can help you:

Cancer Centres and Hospitals:

Most cancer centres and hospitals have dedicated support services such as social workers, patient advisors, and financial counsellors to help you with various forms of support, from emotional counselling to financial assistance.

Patient Navigation

Patient advisors and navigators are trained to help patients with the healthcare system. They help schedule appointments, coordinate care, and access resources.

Patient Support Groups

Cancer support groups help patients connect with others facing similar challenges. They support patients emotionally, help share information, and provide a sense of community. Some are in-person, and others are online or telephone-based to cater to those who cannot attend in person.

Mental Health Services

Psychologists, psychiatrists, and counsellors help patients cope with the emotional toll of cancer with counselling, therapy, and support for anxiety, depression, and other mental health challenges.

Financial Assistance Programs

Many organisations and foundations help cancer patients with financial assistance to cover the costs of treatment, medication, transport, and other expenses. Social workers and financial counsellors at healthcare facilities will guide you in finding and accessing them.

Transport Services

Cancer treatment typically requires frequent medical appointments. Transport services like volunteer driver programs or specialised companies will help you get to and from your appointments.

Home Healthcare Services

You may require home healthcare services like nursing, physical therapy, or palliative care. You can arrange these services through your healthcare provider or support services.

Nutritional Support

Dietitians and nutritionists can guide your diet during treatment and help you manage any side effects.

Physical Therapy and Rehabilitation

Take advantage of physical therapists to help you regain physical strength, mobility, and function after surgery or to overcome treatment-related side effects.

Palliative Care and Hospices

Palliative care improves the quality of life for patients with severe illnesses by managing symptoms and addressing emotional and spiritual needs. Hospice care is for patients nearing the end of their life and focuses on comfort and pain management.

Legal and Financial Services

You will need legal experts to help with advance healthcare directives, disposing of your estate, and addressing employment-related issues. Financial advisors can help you navigate insurance, budgeting, and long-term financial planning.

Complementary and Alternative Therapies

You will probably benefit from complementary therapies like acupuncture, massage, yoga, and meditation. These are often available at cancer centres or through referrals.

Cancer Information and Resources

You can use libraries, online resources, and cancer-specific organisations to find treatment options, clinical trials, and survivorship information.

Community and Non-profit Organisations

Local and national organisations, such as the American Cancer Society, provide support services, including information, transport assistance, financial aid, and support groups; please get in touch with them.

Online Resources and Telehealth Services

Online and telehealth platforms give information, counselling, and support from the comfort of your home. Please find out how to get in touch with them via your healthcare provider, social worker, patient advocate, or cancer support organisations.

Recommendations and Resources

The following are organisations that can help you through your cancer journey:

Patient Advocacy Organisations

Many cancer-focused organisations have financial assistance, educational, and financial management programmes. They include the American Cancer Society, CancerCare, the Macmillan Cancer Support and the Cancer Support Community.

Social Workers and Financial Counsellors

Hospitals and cancer centres typically have social workers and financial advisors to help patients get financial assistance, negotiate medical bills, and create budgets.

Government Programs

During and after treatment, you may qualify for government programmes such as Medicaid, Medicare, Social Security Disability Insurance (SSDI), and Supplemental Security Income (SSI).

Non-profit Organisations

Some non-profit organisations, including the Leukaemia & Lymphoma Society's Patient Financial Aid Program and The Pink Fund, give cancer patients financial help with transport, housing, and medication.

Prescription Assistance Programs

Some pharmaceutical companies have prescription assistance programs that give reduced or free medication to eligible patients.

Cancer-specific Foundations

Some foundations are dedicated to those with specific cancers. For instance, the Multiple Myeloma Research Foundation gives financial help to multiple myeloma patients. Research organisations that help those with your cancer type.

State and Local Resources

State and local resources provide financial, housing, and utility bill help for those with cancer. Ensure you research and take advantage of them.

Legal Aid Services

Some legal aid groups give free or low-cost legal help to address employment, insurance, and financial matters.

Financial Advisors and Planners

Contact your bank or other financial professionals to help with budgeting, debts, and long-term finances.

Employment Assistance Programs

Your employer may offer employee assistance programmes (EAPs) that provide counselling, legal advice, and financial planning services. Ask your boss or human resources department for details.

Local Charities and Religious Organisations

Local charities and religious and community organisations in your area probably help with finances, food, and other support.

Pharmacy Discount Cards

Pharmacy discount cards cut the costs of your medications. They are widely available, and you can use them in conjunction with your health insurance. Ask your local pharmacy.

Financial Aid for Education

There are scholarships and grants for cancer survivors. Ask about them at your local library or educational institution.

Supportive Communities

Finally, online communities and local support groups give invaluable emotional and practical support. They have experience with others in similar situations. Ask your medical team or social worker to put you in touch with those in your area.

The Following is a List of Resources in the US:

American Cancer Society (ACS)

The ACS provides a wealth of information on financial assistance, insurance, and coping with the financial aspects of cancer care. They offer resources, publications, and guidance on managing medical bills, insurance claims, and financial planning.

Website: American Cancer Society - Financial Guidance

Cancer Financial Assistance Coalition (CFAC)

CFAC is a coalition of national organisations that provide financial assistance and support services to cancer patients.

Their website offers a searchable database of financial assistance programs and resources.

Website: CFAC

Patient Advocate Foundation (PAF)

PAF offers case management services and educational resources to help cancer patients deal with insurance and access financial assistance.

Website: Patient Advocate Foundation

CancerCare

CancerCare offers financial assistance, including grants for transport, home care, and co-payments. They also give counselling and provide support groups to help cancer patients with financial and emotional challenges.

Website: CancerCare

The Leukemia & Lymphoma Society (LLS)

LLS offers finance to help blood cancer patients with treatment, transport, and other expenses. They also provide financial education.

Website: LLS Financial Support

Social Security Administration (SSA)

The SSA administers disability benefits, including Social Security Disability Insurance (SSDI) and Supplemental Security Income (SSI), which may be available to those with cancer who cannot work due to their condition.

Website: Social Security Administration

American Institute for Cancer Research (AICR)

AICR gives help with financial and legal matters related to cancer care. They can guide you on health insurance and financial and legal issues.

Website: AICR Financial and Legal Resources

Local Cancer Support Organisations

Many local cancer support and non-profit organisations offer financial assistance and support services to cancer patients within their communities. These organisations typically understand local resources so that they can provide you with tailored assistance.

Online Communities

Joining online cancer communities, forums, or social media groups connects you with others facing financial challenges during and after cancer treatment. Some deal with specific types and stages of cancer, employment statuses, and economic situations.

Help with Medical Bills

The following are ways of obtaining financial help with your medical bills:

Contact Your Healthcare Provider

Contact your healthcare provider or hospital's financial or billing department as soon as possible. Explain your situation and inquire about financial assistance programs or discounts. Some offer sliding-scale fees or charity care for those facing financial hardship. Ask about manageable payment plans.

Review Your Health Insurance Coverage

Review your health insurance terms and conditions for cancer treatment. Check on deductibles, co-payments, and out-of-pocket maximums. Contact your insurance provider to clarify coverage and other aspects you are unsure about. Check if your healthcare provider is in-network, as that maximises your benefits.

Apply for Government Programs

Medicaid: If you have a low income, you probably qualify for Medicaid, a state and federally-funded programme that provides healthcare coverage. Please beware that eligibility varies from state to state.

Medicare: Those over 65 and some younger people with disabilities are usually eligible for Medicare. This federal health insurance program covers many cancer-related expenses.

Affordable Care Act (ACA) Marketplace: Explore insurance and subsidies through the ACA Marketplace, especially if you do not have employer-sponsored insurance.

Appeal Insurance Denials

If your company refuses to pay for some treatments or procedures, you can appeal by following their process. If you have any issues, seek legal advice.

Prescription Assistance Programs

Investigate pharmaceutical company assistance programmes that provide free or reduced-cost medication for cancer treatment. Your healthcare provider or oncologist can often help.

Community Resources

Contact local community organisations, religious institutions, and social services agencies for financial, transportation, and other support sources.

Financial Aid for Clinical Trials

If you are participating in a clinical trial, financial assistance may be available for participants.

Patient Advocacy Groups

Patient advocacy groups dedicated to specific cancer types sometimes offer financial assistance or resources tailored to your cancer type.

Obtaining help for medical bills can be complex. However, some resources and professionals help. Ask patient advocacy groups to guide you in finding who can help you.

Dealing with Finances After a Cancer Diagnosis in the UK

The UK healthcare is publicly funded. This section highlights exceptions and helps guide you towards resources you might need if you are a UK resident.

Because the government funds the NHS in the UK, you may assume that all costs related to cancer care are covered. However, you could still face some financial challenges after being diagnosed with cancer, including travel, prescription charges, out-of-pocket costs, loss of income and adjustments to pension plans.

Financial Challenges in the UK

The following are some typical financial challenges those diagnosed with cancer in the UK experience:

Medical Expenses

Even though the NHS covers most cancer treatment expenses, you, as the patient, must cover some costs, such as prescription charges and dental care.

Travel and Accommodation Expenses

Cancer treatment requires regular visits to hospitals and other healthcare facilities, resulting in travel expenses such as fuel, public transport, and parking. Some patients must travel between cities for specialist treatment and care, which incurs accommodation and food costs.

Loss of Income

Cancer treatment often requires time off or switching to part-time employment, leading to reduced income, especially for those on zero-hour or fixed contracts.

Self-Employed and Small Business Owners

Self-employed or small business-owning cancer patients face even more significant financial challenges because they do not have income security and may not have access to the same employment protections and benefits as employees.

Insurance Gaps

Even though the NHS covers the cost of medical treatment in the UK, some people have health insurance that gives them access to private treatment. That allows them to have access to treatment faster than an NHS patient. However, most cannot afford comprehensive health insurance, so they must personally cover part of their treatment. The cost of co-payments and deductibles leaves many cancer patients in severe financial hardship.

Cost of Living

Many people struggle to cover daily expenses such as rent or mortgage payments, utilities, groceries, and childcare. Adding the challenges brought about by cancer can be overwhelming.

Long-Term Financial Impact

Those who survive cancer are more likely to experience long-term financial challenges, such as difficulty securing employment, higher insurance premiums, and reduced earning potential.

Access to Financial Support in the UK

UK cancer patients have access to many financial support services to help manage the challenges associated with their treatment, including the following:

NHS Funding

The NHS provides free medical treatment for cancer patients. In addition, the NHS and local authorities assist with transport in certain circumstances.

Prescription Prepayment Certificates (PPCs)

Even though many prescriptions are free for UK cancer patients, those who have to pay can access PPCs, which fix prescription fees. The Cancer Drugs Fund (CDF) also covers the cost of cancer drugs not routinely available through the NHS. The CDF ensures patients can access the most effective cancer treatments even if they cannot afford them.

Various Benefits You Could Access

Personal Independence Payment (PIP) is a non-means-tested benefit to cover costs related to daily living and mobility to help those with long-term health conditions, including cancer.

Employment and Support Allowance (ESA), consisting of an assessment phase and a main phase, provides financial assistance to those unable to work due to health conditions, including cancer.

Universal Credit is a means-tested benefit that replaces several other benefits. It is for those on low incomes or unable to work due to health conditions.

Attendance Allowance is a benefit that helps those aged 65 and over with health conditions, including cancer, cover extra care-related costs.

Many **local councils** also offer assistance with housing, council tax, and other finances to cancer patients.

Macmillan Cancer Support offers one-off grants to cancer patients in financial hardship to help them cover costs such as heating bills and clothing.

Many cancer **charities** and organisations, such as **Cancer Research UK**, provide financial support, information, and resources to cancer patients and their families.

Benefit advisors and welfare rights experts can help you access financial support and benefits.

Many **cancer support centres** have financial advisors who help patients understand their financial situation and access support services.

Patient advocacy organisations, like **Macmillan Cancer Support** and **Citizens Advice**, offer information and advice on financial support and benefits.

https://www.macmillan.org.uk/

https://www.citizensadvice.org.uk

Those caring for loved ones with cancer can also access financial support, such as the carer's allowance.

If you need help, ask your healthcare provider, social worker, patient advocate or benefits advisor.

Access to Occupational Health Services:

Employees can access occupational health services that help cancer patients and survivors return to work safely and plan for the necessary adjustments.

Insurance Protection:

All UK employers must have liability insurance covering employees' work-related injuries and illnesses, including cancer.

Financial Support:

Access to Employee Assistance Programs (EAPs)

Many employers in the UK offer EAPs that provide counselling, legal advice, and financial planning services to employees and their families.

You must communicate openly with your employer about your diagnosis and request necessary adjustments or support. Employers are legally obliged to make reasonable adjustments and support employees with cancer.

The UK Benefits System

The UK offers a range of benefits for those diagnosed with cancer. However, navigating the system can be complex.

The following list details the benefits you might be entitled to and how to access them:

Statutory Sick Pay (SSP)

SSP benefits employees too ill to work, including cancer patients. The employer pays it for up to 28 weeks. The employee must be at the lower end of the salary scale and absent from work for at least four consecutive days.

Employment and Support Allowance (ESA)

ESA is available to cancer patients and others unable to work due to illness or disability. It consists of two components: the assessment phase and the main phase. You need a work capability assessment or "fit note" (formerly known as a sick note) from your GP to be eligible.

Personal Independence Payment (PIP)

PIP is a non-means-tested benefit to help those with a long-term health condition or disability cope with extra costs. To apply, you must complete a claim form and attend an assessment. The payment consists of two components: daily living and mobility.

Universal Credit

Universal Credit is a means-tested benefit available to those on low incomes or unable to work due to health conditions. You can apply online.

Attendance Allowance (for those aged 65 and over)

Attendance Allowance is a non-means-tested benefit that pays someone to help those aged 65 and over with personal care because of a health condition, including cancer.

Carer's Allowance

Someone caring for a cancer patient for at least 35 hours a week may be eligible for Carer's Allowance, a means-tested benefit.

You can find get more comprehensive information on the mentionedbenefitsbyclickingthelinkhttps://www.macmillan.

org.uk/cancer-information-and-support/get-help/cost-of-living/understanding-benefits?gclid=cjwkcaianl-sbhbneiwa-jrgighhx5gauvs1mqyed-0ag9pb0u85la08s5xssmbj8gj9dbwp-pifme5hocdhaqavd_bwe&gclsrc=aw.ds or by following the guidelines presented below.

The following are tips for successfully navigating the UK benefits system:

Contact a cancer support organisation or charity, such as Macmillan Cancer Support or Citizens Advice, for guidance on the benefits available and assistance with the application process.

Consult your GP and request a "fit note" (formerly a sick note) to support your benefit applications.

Keep accurate records of medical appointments, treatments, and related expenses, as this information may be needed when applying for benefits.

Seek help from Citizens Advice to understand your rights and eligibility for benefits.

Apply for your benefits as soon as possible, meet the application deadlines and provide all necessary documentation.

Please be aware that the criteria and processes change constantly. So, stay informed by checking official government websites and seeking advice from reputable sources.

UK-Based Resources

Beyond the information in this book, many UK-based resources help people manage their finances after a cancer diagnosis, including Macmillan Cancer Support, Citizens Advice, and government websites.

Macmillan Cancer Support is the UK's leading cancer support organisation. They provide financial guidance and support, including information on benefits, grants, and practical advice.

Website: Macmillan Cancer Support

Citizens Advice offers free and confidential advice on benefits, debt management, and financial support for cancer patients.

Website: Citizens Advice

The National Health Service (NHS) website gives information about prescription charges, travel expenses and help with costs.

Website: NHS Financial Help

Department for Work and Pensions (DWP) administers Personal Independence Payment (PIP), Employment and Support Allowance (ESA), and Disability Living Allowance (DLA).

Website: DWP

Cancer Research UK provides information and resources on financial support for UK cancer patients and guidance on benefits and financial assistance programmes.

Website: Cancer Research UK - Financial Support

The Money Advice Service offers free, impartial advice about managing money during a health crisis.

Website: The Money Advice Service

Financial Help:

Finding help to pay private medical bills in the UK is challenging. The following are some helpful hints:

Check Your Private Health Insurance

Review the terms and conditions of your private insurance or contact them to verify the extent of your coverage. You can appeal the decision if your private health insurance denies coverage for a particular treatment or procedure. Use the company's appeal process.

Discuss Payment Plans

Private healthcare providers are always open to negotiating payment plans. You can request an instalment plan that spreads the cost over several months or even years.

Seek Support from Charities and Non-profit Organisations

Some UK charities and non-profit organisations help to finance private medical bills. Contact them and ask.

Consider Legal Protection

Research the laws and regulations regarding debt collection and consumer rights. If you are unsure, ask Citizens Advice.

Help from Friends and Family

Discuss your situation with friends and family who might help you cover your medical bills.

Debt Management Services

If you have problems paying your medical bills, talk to your bank, a debt management service or counsellors who will help you negotiate with your creditors.

Please remember private healthcare providers have different policies and options concerning bills. Communicate openly and honestly with them about your circumstances and ability to pay.

ACTION PLAN

Step 1

Research your employment rights. You have specific rights when you are unwell. Check your company's policies concerning sick leave, disability leave and flexible work arrangements.

Step 2

Tell your employer about your diagnosis and treatment so they can make allowances. They might permit you to work remotely, work reduced hours or allow you a leave of absence.

Step 3

Get a financial advisor to assess your situation and plan for changes in income. Create a budget that accounts for extra expenses and possible loss of income.

Step 4

Review your health insurance policy for your treatment and medication cover. Budget for any extra costs like travel and overnight stays.

Step 5

Seek financial help from the government, charities, and patient advocacy groups. Many benefits are available for those in your circumstances, especially if you are incapacitated and cannot work. Consider crowdfunding or community fundraisers if necessary.

Step 6

Tell your family and friends about your circumstances and any support you need. If your employer has a help programme, take advantage of it.

Step 7

Everyone in your support network might be capable of helping in different ways. So, play to the strength of each person and spread the burden.

Step 8

Maintain a good work-life balance. If you die, your work will continue, so prioritise your health over your work. Tell your employer how you are coping and schedule rest and naps in your day.

Step 9

You might need legal help with your commitments.

Step 10

Take advantage of assistance programmes from cancer organisations for managing work, finances, and relationships during treatment.

Step 11

Regularly review your financial situation, work arrangements, and relationship dynamics, and make adjustments if necessary.

Step 12

Maintain a record of all your medical reports, appointments, finances, insurance information, and work correspondence.

Step 13:

Communicate regularly with your employer, insurance company, financial advisors, and support network.

____

____

____

____

____

____

____

____

Chapter Ten:
How to Avoid Cancer Recurrence

There is no underestimating the significance of ringing the bell when your cancer treatment is over. It marks a massive milestone in your life. The end of active cancer treatment marks a profound psychological and emotional transition from a patient under constant care and scrutiny to a new phase in their life: survivorship. However, this phase is as challenging and transformative as the treatment.

Cancer is a life-altering event that involves intensive treatments, emotional upheaval, and significant changes. For some, cancer diagnosis and treatment are the most life-altering events they have ever had to deal with, so completing the treatment leaves a massive void in their lives. While some might embrace the opportunity of a new life, others view it with trepidation. The reality is this: you will never be the same person you were before cancer. You need to consider this period an opportunity to start your life over again.

For some, cancer diagnosis and treatment are the most life-altering events they have ever had to deal with, so completing the treatment leaves a massive void in their lives

The Transition Process from Patient to Survivor

The following are some steps you can take to make a smooth transition from patient to survivor:

Create A Survivorship Care Plan

Your healthcare team will work with you to create a survivorship plan that contains your treatment history, potential late side effects, and a regular follow-up schedule. Do not be deluded; cancer does reoccur, that's why it is vital to develop an active survivorship plan. It is your roadmap for post-treatment life, with guidance on how to deal with potential late or lingering side effects and how to manage your recovery and post-cancer healthcare actively.

A practical survivorship plan contains the following:

- information about your cancer diagnosis and treatment history,
- your schedule for follow-up care and screenings,
- details of possible late effects or complications related to your treatment,
- suggestions about lifestyle choices

Acknowledge the Reality

Acknowledging your new status is essential to the journey. It involves the dichotomy of coming to terms with the physical and emotional toll of diagnosis and treatment while simultaneously celebrating your strength and resilience for getting through it.

Post-Cancer Treatment Emotions

Surviving cancer brings a range of mixed emotions, including relief, anxiety, fear, and uncertainty. It helps to view these emotions as a part of the transition and healing process.

One way of dealing with the complex emotions after cancer treatment is cultivating your support network. Share your thoughts and feelings with your friends, family, and support groups. If you find the experience overwhelming, try professional counselling or therapy. The emotional aspects of cancer are as challenging as the physical aspects. Be honest with yourself and give your emotions the time and space they need to settle down. Approach the process with self-compassion and openness, and get support from those around you. Many cancer survivors use mindfulness meditation, yoga, journaling, or creative outlets like art and music.

Some practical post-cancer strategies are making lifestyle adjustments and re-evaluating your priorities. The following also needs to be included:

Reflection

Take time to reflect on what truly matters to you. You may discover that your life's direction, purpose, and priorities have shifted due to your cancer journey.

Set New Goals

Set clear, achievable goals encompassing your career, family, personal development, and overall well-being. That will give you a new sense of purpose and control.

Work-Life Balance

Evaluate your work-life balance and ensure it supports your physical and emotional health. If that is not the case, make bold changes.

Supportive Relationships

Surround yourself with friends and family who understand and empathise with your journey to recovery. Please share your thoughts, feelings, and concerns with them. Open communication strengthens ties and provides emotional support. Cultivating and maintaining supportive relationships is a valuable part of survivorship.

Maintaining Physical Health

The key to preventing cancer from recurring is changing your lifestyle. That includes ensuring a healthy diet, regular physical activity, and avoiding negative behaviours that compromise your immune system. Eating a well-balanced diet rich in fruits, vegetables, lean proteins, and whole grains gives you the necessary nutrients for complete recovery. Physical activity, however moderate, is essential for boosting your energy levels, improving your mood, and helping you manage your treatment's side effects.

It is also worth bearing in mind that you might have late effects. As a cancer survivor, chances are you may experience some late effects of your treatment. These could appear months or even years after treatment has finished. They include fatigue, neuropathy, cognitive changes, or the development of secondary cancers. That is why regular check-ups, including tests and screenings, are essential. Regular communication with your healthcare team, discussing any symptoms or concerns, and being proactive about your health provide the opportunity for timely interventions. Adopting a healthy lifestyle improves your physical and emotional well-being. It is also a positive step towards regaining control and fostering a hopeful outlook.

Physical Rehabilitation

Strength training is vital for muscular function, especially after cancer treatment. Ask your healthcare provider about exercise, physiotherapy, and specific dietary plans.[127]

Psychological Rehabilitation

Cancer treatment also results in immense emotional and psychological trauma. Therefore, it's crucial to maintain counselling, therapy, and participation in your support groups. That is especially important if you underwent a surgical procedure that left you with scars on your body.[128]

Social Rehabilitation

Even though cancer changes you, it is vital you re-integrate into society after treatment. As easy as that might sound, it is not so easy to reengage with friends and families or work colleagues after experiencing such a traumatic life-altering event. You need to make a sustained effort to orient yourself to your world again.[129]

The Ever Present Fear of Recurrence

The possibility of cancer recurrence will remain a looming shadow in your mind even as you celebrate recovery. Although such a traumatic event will probably stay with you for the rest of your life, your fear must become a reference, not a resident in your mind.

The following are steps to maintain vigilance without being paralysed by constant fear:

Understanding the Fear

Being hyper-vigilant after such a traumatic event is natural, but don't be alarmed by every little bodily change or symptom. The reoccurrence of cancer is not inevitable.[130]

Constructive Vigilance

A healthy lifestyle is the antidote to the fear of cancer reoccurrence. Go for regular check-ups, stick to medical advice, lead a healthy lifestyle, eat a healthy diet, exercise regularly, and maintain a close social circle.[131]

Strategies for Coping Emotionally

Practising yoga, meditation, mindfulness, and cognitive-behavioural therapy are all effective ways of maintaining equilibrium and managing anxieties related to cancer recurrence.[132]

Understanding that survivorship begins at the end of cancer treatment is vital, but it does not end there. Understanding that it is a continuum lasting a lifetime is critical to avoiding cancer recurrence. Prioritise physical and emotional well-being through a healthy lifestyle, support networks, and self-care practices. Commit to regular follow-ups to monitor for late effects and maintain overall health. Embrace lifestyle adjustments and re-evaluate your life priorities to align them with your values and goals. You don't just necessarily need to survive; you can also strive and thrive.

Key Points

Join Survivorship Programmes

Engage in survivorship programmes your healthcare provider and cancer organisations offer for educational resources, support groups, and care plans.

Join Support Groups

Connect with cancer survivor support groups. Sharing stories, insights, and challenges with others provides vital emotional support.

Be Your Own Advocate

Actively participate in your healthcare decisions and advocate for yourself. Ask questions and express yourself to your healthcare professionals.

Stay Up to Date

Keep yourself informed about the latest research and insights into survivorship, make informed decisions, and access cutting-edge treatments and support.

Mark Milestones

Celebrate big and small milestones in your survivorship journey to add inspiration and motivation.

Nurture Your Supportive Network

Surround yourself with loved ones and fellow survivors to find comfort and understanding and enrich your emotional health.

Find New Interests

Explore new interests and hobbies to inspire you and help your overall well-being.

Find Meaning

Giving back to your community is an excellent source of meaning and purpose. Volunteer or become an advocate to support others facing similar challenges.

Useful Resources for Survivorship

Your healthcare provider and many cancer organisations have survivorship programmes to support people in your position. They include:

Educational Resources: provide access to educational materials and workshops for survivors to better understand the next phase of their recovery.

Support Groups: help survivors interact with other survivors, share experiences, and get emotional support.

Survivorship Care Plans: include a schedule of follow-up care, late-effect monitoring, and lifestyle recommendations.

Online Communities

Join Online Communities: Online communities and forums help survivors to connect with others, share insights, and seek advice. Some popular cancer survivorship communities include:

Cancer Survivors Network: A forum for survivors to discuss various survivorship, treatment, and recovery topics.

Cancer Support Community: offers various resources, including discussion boards and webinars.

Cancer Survivorship Organisations

There are many organisations dedicated to offering a wealth of information, resources, and programmes to cancer survivors, including the following:

American Cancer Society (ACS) gives wide-ranging information on survivorship, including managing physical and emotional health, creating care plans, and finding support.

National Cancer Institute (NCI) has a comprehensive guide to survivorship, covering topics like managing physical and emotional health, including late effects.

Professional Support

Professional support for cancer survivors includes the following:

Licensed Counsellors and Therapists can help you address emotional challenges, anxiety, depression, and other psychological challenges.

Dietitians and Nutritionists help cancer survivors maintain a healthy diet and manage nutritional challenges.

Physical Therapists help cancer survivors with exercises and strategies to improve their physical well-being.

Supportive Care Specialists help survivors manage the late effects of cancer treatment and improve their overall quality of life.

The Road Ahead

As difficult as the cancer journey is, survivorship is an opportunity for personal growth, resilience, and appreciation for life. Remember that hope is a good thing, and good things never die.

Embrace each day with gratitude and an appreciation for your life. Develop a growth mindset and share your experiences to inspire and support others. Cancer is a part of your past; it does not have to define your future. Remember, you can start your world over again; embrace it.

ACTION PLAN

Step 1

Ensure you strictly adhere to the post-treatment schedule.

Step 2

Adopt a healthy diet rich in fruits, vegetables, whole grains, and lean proteins, and avoid processed foods and sugars.

Step 3

Maintain a healthy weight through diet and exercise.

Step 4

Exercise regularly. Seek advice and recommendations from your healthcare team and support network.

Step 5

Reduce or preferably eliminate alcohol consumption. Alcohol increases the risk of some cancers.

Step 6

Stop smoking. Like alcohol, there is a direct link between tobacco and some cancers.

Step 7

Develop your ability to manage stress. Enrol in stress management activities like mindfulness, yoga, and meditation.

Step 8

Get adequate, quality sleep every night. Sleep is critical to healing and maintaining a healthy immune system.

Step 9

Monitor new symptoms and changes in your health. If you experience anything alarming, get in touch with your healthcare team immediately.

Step 10

Keep up to date with new research and treatments for preventing cancer recurrence.

Step 11

Continue taking your medication as directed by your healthcare provider. They prescribed them for good reason.

Step 12

Avoid environmental risks by minimising your exposure to known carcinogens.

Step 13

Stay up to date with information about your type of cancer, innovative ways of preventing recurrence, and the latest screening methods.

Step 14

Use holistic and complementary therapies that support your overall well-being.

Step 15

Your family, friends, healthcare providers, and fellow survivors are vital sources of encouragement and support, so enlist them in your preventive efforts.

Step 16

Develop a personalised, long-term, healthy lifestyle plan with strategies for maintaining your health and monitoring danger signs. Ask your healthcare provider, support network, and survivor groups for help.

Useful Resources

References for UK Residents

Books and Publications:

"Living with and Beyond Cancer: Taking Action to Improve Outcomes." National Cancer Survivorship Initiative (NCSI) (This is also available online)

"The UK Way Forward: A Cancer Strategy for the Next Generation." Macmillan Cancer Support (This is also available online).

Organisations:

Macmillan Cancer Support

Website: Macmillan Cancer Support

Cancer Research UK

Website: Cancer Research UK

NHS Cancer Services

Website: NHS Cancer Services

Cancer Survivorship UK

Website: Cancer Survivorship UK

Support and Survivorship Organisations:

Maggie's Centres.

Website: Maggie's Centres

Teenage Cancer Trust.

Website: Teenage Cancer Trust

CLIC Sargent.

Website: CLIC Sargent

Government Health Agencies:

NHS England - Cancer

Website: NHS England - Cancer

Public Health England - Cancer Services

Website: Public Health England - Cancer Services

Macmillan Cancer Support - Information for Healthcare Professionals

Website: Macmillan Cancer Support - Healthcare Professionals

Patient Advocacy Groups:

Beating Bowel Cancer

Website: Beating Bowel Cancer

Brain Tumour Research

Website: Brain Tumour Research

Academic and Medical Institutions:

The Christie NHS Foundation Trust - Survivorship Programme

Website: The Christie Survivorship Programme

University College London Hospitals NHS Foundation Trust - Cancer Survivorship Programme

Website: UCLH Cancer Survivorship Programme

Useful References for US Residents:

Books and Publications:

"The American Cancer Society's Survivorship Care Compendium." American Cancer Society

Website: American Cancer Society - Survivorship Care Compendium

"Living Beyond Cancer: Finding a New Balance." National Cancer Institute.

Online Publication: Living Beyond Cancer: Finding a New Balance

"The Cancer Survivor's Companion: Practical Ways to Cope with Your Feelings After Cancer" by Dr. Frances Goodhart and Lucy Atkins.

Book: The Cancer Survivor's Companion

"Cancer Survivorship: Next Steps for Patients and Their Families." National Cancer Institute.

Online Publication: "Cancer Survivorship: Next Steps for Patients and Their Families."

Organisations:

American Cancer Society (ACS)

Website: American Cancer Society

National Cancer Institute (NCI)

Website: National Cancer Institute

Cancer.Net

Website: Cancer.Net

Cancer Support Community

Website: Cancer Support Community

CancerCare

Website: CancerCare

Support and Survivorship Organisations:

The LIVESTRONG Foundation

Website: LIVESTRONG Foundation

Susan G. Komen Breast Cancer Foundation

Website: Susan G. Komen

Leukemia & Lymphoma Society (LLS)

Website: Leukemia & Lymphoma Society

Stupid Cancer

Website: Stupid Cancer

Government Health Agencies:

Center for Disease Control and Prevention (CDC) - Cancer Survivorship

Website: CDC - Cancer Survivorship

National Cancer Institute (NCI) - Office of Cancer Survivorship

Website: NCI - Office of Cancer Survivorship

Agency for Healthcare Research and Quality (AHRQ) - Cancer Survivorship

Website: AHRQ - Cancer Survivorship

Patient Advocacy Groups:

American Cancer Society Cancer Action Network (ACS CAN)

Website: ACS CAN

National Coalition for Cancer Survivorship (NCCS)

Website: NCCS

Academic and Medical Institutions:

Memorial Sloan Kettering Cancer Center - Cancer Survivorship Program

Website: MSK Cancer Survivorship Program

MD Anderson Cancer Center - Cancer Survivorship Program

Website: MD Anderson Cancer Survivorship

More Resources for People Diagnosed with Cancer:

Support Groups:

American Cancer Society's Cancer Survivors Network is a community of survivors and caregivers where one can share personal experiences and stories.

Gilda's Club, named after comedian Gilda Radner, is a network offering social and emotional support.

CancerCare is an association offering free support, information, financial assistance, and practical help to those with cancer and their loved ones.

The Leukemia & Lymphoma Society's Community is a community specifically for individuals with blood cancers to connect and share.

Books:

"The Emperor of All Maladies: A Biography of Cancer" by Siddhartha Mukherjee is a comprehensive history of cancer and its impact on humanity.

"When Breath Becomes Air" by Paul Kalanithi is a memoir by a young neurosurgeon faced with terminal lung cancer.

"Anti-Cancer: A New Way of Life" by David Servan-Schreiber explores the science and strategies that can slow down cancer's progression.

"Living with Cancer: A Step-by-Step Guide for Coping Medically and Emotionally with a Serious Diagnosis" by Vicki A. Jackson and David P. Ryan is a practical guide for patients and caregivers.

Relevant Websites:

National Cancer Institute (NCI) at https://www.cancer.gov/

provides up-to-date information on various cancers, treatments, and research.

Cancer.Net at https://www.cancer.net/, produced by the American Society of Clinical Oncology (ASCO), offers patient-centered information on various cancers.

Breastcancer.org at https://www.breastcancer.org/ is a resource dedicated to breast cancer information and support.

Cancer Research UK at https://www.cancerresearchuk.org/ offers information about cancer, research updates, and support resources.

Glossary

Adjuvant Therapy is a treatment given after the primary treatment to increase the chances of a cure. It might include chemo, radiation, or hormone therapy.

Alternative Therapies are treatments used in place of standard medical treatments. Examples include specific diets or the use of herbs.

Benign or non-cancerous tumours do not grow uncontrollably, invade neighbouring tissues, or spread throughout the body.

Chemotherapy is a cancer treatment that uses one or more anti-cancer drugs as part of a standardised regimen.

Carcinoma is a cancer that starts in cells that make up the skin or the tissues that line organs.

Diagnosis identifies a disease or condition by evaluating symptoms, signs, and patient history.

External Radiation is a treatment that uses a machine to direct high-energy rays or particles at the cancer from outside the body.

Hormone Therapy is a treatment that adds, blocks or removes hormones to slow or stop the growth of cancer cells.

Holistic Therapies are treatment approaches that take into account the whole person, including their physical, emotional, mental, and spiritual well-being. Examples include meditation and acupuncture.

Immunotherapy is a cancer treatment that boosts the body's natural defences to fight cancer.

Lymph Nodes are small, bean-shaped organs that produce and store cells that fight infection.

Malignant or cancerous cells that can invade and destroy nearby tissues and spread to other parts of the body.

Metastasis is the spread of cancer cells from where they first formed to another part of the body.

Palliative Care is specialized medical care that focuses on relieving the symptoms and stress of serious illnesses to improve the quality of life for the patient and their family.

Radiation Therapy uses high doses of radiation to destroy or damage cancer cells.

Remission is a decrease in or disappearance of signs and symptoms of cancer.

Support Groups consist of people who share a common condition or experience and provide emotional and moral support to each other.

Survivors are people who remain alive and continue to function during and after overcoming a severe hardship or life-threatening disease.

Targeted Therapy is a treatment that uses drugs to identify and attack specific types of cancer cells with less harm to normal cells.

Tumours are masses formed when normal cells begin to change and grow uncontrollably.[133, 134]

Reference

[1] Centers for Disease Control and Prevention. Cancer Deaths. [online]. [June 26, 2023; Accessed October 9, 2023]. Available from: https://www.cdc.gov/nchs/hus/topics/cancer-deaths.htm

[2] Hassan C. Cancer death rates fall steadily in the US, with more survivors than ever. [online]. [September 21, 2022]; Accessed October 9, 2023]. Available from: https://edition.cnn.com/2022/09/21/health/cancer-deaths-decline-research-report/index.html

[3] American Cancer Society. Survival Rates for prostate cancer. [online]. [Accessed October 9, 2023]. Available from: https://www.cancer.org/cancer/types/prostate-cancer/detection-diagnosis-staging/survival-rates.html

[4] American Cancer Society. 5 year relative survival. [online]. [Accessed October 9, 2023]. Available from: https://cancerstatisticscenter.cancer.org/#/

[5] Ibid American Cancer Society. 5 year relative survival.

[6] American Cancer Society. Adjusting to life with cancer. [online]. [Accessed October 9, 2023]. Available from: https://www.cancer.org/cancer/survivorship/coping/adjusting-to-life-with-cancer.html

[7] Spiegel D, Moore RJ. Imagery and hypnosis in the treatment of cancer patients. *Oncology*. [Internet].1997 Aug. [Cited

December 18, 2023]. 11(8): 1179-1190. Available from: https://www.researchgate.net/publication/233742461_Spiegel_D_Moore_RJ_1997_Imagery_and_Hypnosis_in_the_Treatment_of_Cancer_Patients_Oncology_11_1179-1190

[8] Cordova M, Riba MB, Spiegel D. Post-traumatic stress disorder and cancer. *Lancet Psychiatry*. [Internet]. 2017 Apr. [Cited December 18, 2023]. 4(4):330-330-8. doi:10.1016/S2215-0366(17)30014-7

[9] Shear MK, Simon N, Wall M, Zisook S, Neimeyer R, Duan N, et al. Complicated grief and related bereavement issues for DSM-5. *Depress Anxiety*. [Internet]. 2011 Feb. [Cited December 18, 2023]. 28(2):103-17. doi:10.1002/da.20780

[10] Carlson LE, Speca M, Patel KD, Goodey E. Mindfulness-based stress reduction in relation to quality of life, mood, symptoms of stress and levels of cortisol, dehydroepiandrosterone sulfate (DHEAS) and melatonin in breast and prostate cancer outpatients. *Psychoneuroendocrinology*. [Internet]. 2004 May. [Cited December 18, 2023]. 29(4):448-74. doi.org/10.1016/S0306-4530(03)00054-4

[11] Mandlik GV, Siopis G, Nguyen B, Ding D, Edwards KM. Effect of a single session of yoga and meditation on stress reactivity: A systematic review. *Stress and Health*. [Internet]. 2023 Oct 11. [Cited December 18, 2023]. doi:10.1002/smi.3324

[12] Craft LL, Perna FM. The Benefits of Exercise for the Clinically Depressed. *Prim Care Companion CNS Disord*. [Internet]. 2004 Jun 1 [Accessed December 18, 2023]. 6(3). doi:10.4088/PCC.v06n0301

[13] Smith S, Anderson-Hanley C, Langrock A, Compas B. The effects of journaling for women with newly diagnosed

breast cancer. *Psycho-Oncology*. [Internet]. 2005 Dec. [Cited December 18, 2023]. 14(12):1075-82. doi:10.1002/pon.912

[14] Hilliard RE. The effect of music therapy sessions on compassion fatigue and team building of professional hospice caregivers. *Arts Psychother*. [Internet]. 2006 Jan. [Cited December 18, 2023]. 33(5):395-401. doi:10.1016/j.aip.2006.06.002

[15] National Cancer Institute. What is cancer? [online]. [October 11, 2021; Accessed October 10, 2023]. Available from: https://www.cancer.gov/about-cancer/understanding/what-is-cancer#:~:text=Cancer%20is%20a%20disease%20caused,sections%20of%20DNA%20called%20genes.

[16] City of Hope. Cancer cell vs. normal cell. [online]. [November 15, 2021; Accessed October 10, 2023]. Available from: https://www.cancercenter.com/cancer-cells-vs-normal-cells#:~:text=The%20human%20body%20constantly%20produces,to%20reproduce%20other%20abnormal%20cells.

[17] Robert Wood Johnson University Hospital. Dictionary of cancer terms. [online]. [Accessed October 10, 2023]. Available from: https://www.rwjbh.org/rwj-university-hospital-somerset/treatment-care/cancer/about/dictionary-of-cancer-terms/

[18] National Library of Medicine. Breast cancer treatment. [online]. [December 2, 2023; Accessed December 28, 2023]. Available from: https://www.ncbi.nlm.nih.gov/books/NBK65969/

[19] National Cancer Institute. Cancer staging. [online]. [October 14, 2022; Accessed October 10, 2023]. Available from:

https://www.cancer.gov/about-cancer/diagnosis-staging/staging

[20] American Cancer Society. Cancer staging. [online]. [Accessed October 10, 2023]. Available from: https://www.cancer.org/cancer/diagnosis-staging/staging.html#:~:text=-Clinical%20staging&text=The%20clinical%20stage%20is%20often,of%20diagnosis%20(see%20below).

[21] MD Anderson Cancer Center. Cancer grade vs. cancer stage. [online]. [Accessed October 10, 2023]. Available from: https://www.mdanderson.org/patients-family/diagnosis-treatment/a-new-diagnosis/cancer-grade-vs--cancer-stage.html#:~:text=Lower%20grade%20cancers%20are%20typically,called%20poorly%20differentiated%20or%20undifferentiated.

[22] National Cancer Institute. Pathology reports. [online]. [August 8, 2022; Accessed October 13, 2023]. Available from: https://www.cancer.gov/about-cancer/diagnosis-staging/diagnosis/pathology-reports-fact-sheet#:~:text=It%20typically%20includes%20a%20gross,provides%20the%20definitive%20cancer%20diagnosis.

[23] Martel L. Embracing Cancer—Embracing Life: The Guide for the Journey Beyond Diagnosis. United States: AuthorHouse; 2015.

[24] John Hopkins Medicine. Study suggests medical errors now third leading cause of death in the U.S. [May 6, 2016; Accessed December 2, 2023]. Available from: https://www.hopkinsmedicine.org/news/media/releases/study_suggests_medical_errors_now_third_leading_cause_of_death_in_the_us

[25] Florida State University. Patient safety definitions. [online]. [Accessed October 11, 2023]. Available from: https://med.fsu.edu/patientsafety/patientSafetyDefinitions

[26] Hillen MA, Medendorp NM, Daams JG, Smets EM. Patient-driven second opinions in oncology: A systematic review. *The Oncologist.* [Internet] 2017 Oct 1. [Cited October 11, 2023]. 22(10):1197-211. doi:10.1634/theoncologist.2016-0429

[27] Ibid Hillen MA, Medendorp NM, Daams JG, Smets EM.

[28] Clauson J, Hsieh YC, Acharya S et al. Results of the Lynn Sage second-opinion program for local therapy in patients with breast carcinoma. Changes in management and determinants of where care is delivered. *Cancer.* [Internet]. 2002. [Cited October 11, 2023]. 94:889–894. doi:10.1002/cncr.10318

[29] RCCA. Two RCCA oncologists explain when and why cancer patients should obtain a second opinion. [online]. [May 11, 2022; Accessed October 11, 2023]. Available from: https://www.regionalcancercare.org/news/two-rcca-oncologists-explain-when-and-why-cancer-patients-should-obtain-a-second-opinion/

[30] Steele C. How much does it cost to see a private consultant in the UK? [online]. [November 1, 2023]; Accessed November 4, 2023]. Available from: https://www.mytribeinsurance.co.uk/treatment/cost-to-see-a-private-consultant-uk

[31] Irish Cancer Society. Getting a second opinion. [online]. [Accessed November 4, 2023]. Available from: https://www.cancer.ie/cancer-information-and-support/cancer-support/coping-with-cancer/information-for-patients/treatment-tips/getting-a-second-opinion

[32] Wikipedia. History of chemotherapy. [online]. [Accessed November 4, 2023]. Available from: https://en.wikipedia.org/wiki/History_of_cancer_chemotherapy#:~:text=The%20era%20of%20cancer%20chemotherapy,the%20early%20researchers%20still%20apply.

[33] NHS. Chemotherapy. [May 25, 2023; Accessed October 13, 2023]. Available from: https://www.nhs.uk/conditions/chemotherapy/

[34] Ibid NHS. Chemotherapy.

[35] Cancer.Net. Nervous system side effects. [online]. [February 2018; Accessed October 13, 2023]. Available from: https://www.cancer.net/coping-with-cancer/physical-emotional-and-social-effects-cancer/managing-physical-side-effects/nervous-system-side-effects

[36] National Cancer Institute. Radiation therapy to treat cancer. [online]. [Accessed October 13, 2023]. Available from: https://www.cancer.gov/about-cancer/treatment/types/radiation-therapy

[37] American Cancer Society. The science behind radiation therapy. [October 27, 2014; Accessed October 13, 2023]. [online]. Available from: https://www.cancer.org/content/dam/CRC/PDF/Public/6151.00.pdf

[38] National Cancer Institute. Radiation therapy to treat cancer. (n 36)

[39] American Cancer Society. The science behind radiation therapy. (n 37)

[40] America Cancer Society. Second cancers related to treatment. [online]. [February 1, 2020; Accessed October 13, 2023].

Available from: https://www.cancer.org/cancer/survivorship/long-term-health-concerns/second-cancers-in-adults/treatment-risks.html

[41] National Cancer Institute. Radiation therapy side effects. [online]. [January 11, 2022; Accessed October 13, 2020]. Available from: https://www.cancer.gov/about-cancer/treatment/types/radiation-therapy/side-effects

[42] National Cancer Institute. Skin and nail changes during cancer treatment. [online]. [December 29, 2022; Accessed October 13, 2023]. Available from: https://www.cancer.gov/about-cancer/treatment/side-effects/skin-nail-changes

[43] NHS. Radiotherapy. [online]. [November 14, 2023; Accessed November 17, 2023]. Available from: https://www.nhsinform.scot/tests-and-treatments/non-surgical-procedures/radiotherapy#side-effects

[43] NHS. Radiotherapy. (n 43)

[44] National Cancer Institute. Radiation therapy side effects. (n 41)

[45] Cancer.Net. What is immunotherapy? [online]. [May 2022; Accessed October 14, 2023]. Available from: https://www.cancer.net/navigating-cancer-care/how-cancer-treated/immunotherapy-and-vaccines/what-immunotherapy#monoclonal-antibodies-immune-checkpoint-inhibitors

[46] Collins BG. What people with cancer should know about immune checkpoint inhibitor side effects. [online]. [November 1, 2021; Accessed October 14, 2023]. Available from: https://www.cancer.net/blog/2021-11/

what-people-with-cancer-should-know-about-immune-checkpoint-inhibitor-side-effects

[47] Cancer.Net. What are cancer vaccines? [online]. [August 2020; Accessed October 14, 2023]. Available from: https://www.cancer.net/navigating-cancer-care/how-cancer-treated/immunotherapy-and-vaccines/what-are-cancer-vaccines

[48] Cancer.Net. What is immunotherapy? (n 45)

[49] Cancer.Net. What are cancer vaccines? (n 47)

[50] Cancer.Net. What is immunotherapy? (n 45)

[51] John Hopkins Medicine. Immunotherapy: precision medicine in action. [online]. [Accessed October 14, 2023]. Available from: https://www.hopkinsmedicine.org/inhealth/about-us/immunotherapy-precision-medicine-action-policy-brief#:~:text=Immunotherapy%20drugs%20work%20better%20in,are%20about%2015%20to%2020%25.

[52] Cancer.Net. What is cancer surgery? [online]. [June 2023; Accessed October 14, 2023]. Available from: https://www.cancer.net/navigating-cancer-care/how-cancer-treated/surgery/what-cancer-surgery#:~:text=Cancer%20surgery%20is%20an% 20operation,is%20called%20a%20surgical%20oncologist.

[53] Cancer Council. What to expect when you return home. [online]. [Accessed October 17, 2023]. Available from: https://www.cancercouncil.com.au/cancer-information/cancer-treatment/surgery/recovery/how-to-plan-for-recovery-at-home/#:~:text=Get%20plenty%20of%20sleep%20and,swimming%2C%20driving%20or%20sexual%20intercourse

[54] American Heart Association. The dangers within: how blood clots affect your health. [online]. [Accessed October 17, 2023]. Available from: https://www.heart.org/en/university-hospitals-harrington-heart-and-vascular/the-dangers-within-how-blood-clots-affect-your-health#:~:text=A%20blood%20clot%2C%20or%20thrombus,it%20can%20cause%20a%20stroke.

[55] American cancer society. Risks of cancer surgery. [online]. [October 2, 2019; Accessed October 17, 2023].Available from: https://www.cancer.org/cancer/managing-cancer/treatment-types/surgery/risks-of-cancer-surgery.html

[56] American Heart Association. The dangers within: how blood clots affect your health. (n 54)

[57] American cancer society. Risks of cancer surgery. (n 55)

[58] UVA Health. Infection after surgery: signs & prevention. [online]. [Accessed October 17, 2023]. Available from: https://uvahealth.com/patients-visitors/prevent-infection-surgery

[59] American cancer society. Risks of cancer surgery. (n 55)

[60] Drugs.com. Postoperative bleeding. [online]. [December 11, 2023; Accessed December 13, 2023]. Available from: https://www.drugs.com/cg/postoperative-bleeding.html

[61] American cancer society. (n 55)

[62] American cancer society. (n 55)

[63] Tohme S, Simmons RL, Tsung A. Surgery for cancer: a trigger for metastases. *Cancer Res.* [Internet]. 2017 Apr. [Cited October 18, 2023]. 77(7):1548-52. doi:10.1158/0008-5472.CAN-16-1536

[64] Brielle G. Improvements in surgery for cancer: the 2020 advance of the year. [online]. [February 4, 2020; Accessed October 18, 2023]. Available from: https://www.cancer.net/blog/2020-02/improvements-surgery-cancer-2020-advance-year

[65] Cancer.Net. Melanoma: introduction. [online]. [Accessed October 18, 2023]. Available from: https://www.cancer.net/cancer-types/melanoma/introduction

[66] Brielle G. Improvements in surgery for cancer: the 2020 advance of the year. (n 64)

[67] Brielle G. Improvements in surgery for cancer: the 2020 advance of the year. (n 64)

[68] Rock CL, Doyle C, Demark-Wahnefried W, Meyerhardt J, Courneya KS, Schwartz AL, et al. Nutrition and physical activity guidelines for cancer survivors. *CA A Cancer J Clinicians*. [Internet] 2012 Jul. [Cited October 18, 2023]. 62(4):242-74. doi.org/10.3322/caac.21142

[69] Morgan K. Constipation during chemotherapy: causes and treatments. [online]. [March 8, 2019; Accessed October 18, 2023]. Available from: https://www.healthline.com/health/breast-cancer-navigator/managing-constipation

[70] Fletcher J. Anti-inflammatory diet: what to know. [online]. [September 6, 2023; Accessed October 25, 2023]. Available from: https://www.medicalnewstoday.com/articles/320233#:~:text=Eating%20less%20processed%20food%2C%20alcohol,examples%20of%20anti%2Dinflammatory%20diets.

[71] American Cancer Society. Loss of appetite. [online]. [September 14, 2022; Accessed October 25, 2023]. Available from: https://www.cancer.org/cancer/managing-cancer/side-effects/eating-problems/poor-appetite.html

[72] Mishra SI, Scherer RW, Snyder C, Geigle P, Gotay C. Are exercise programs effective for improving health-related quality of life among cancer survivors? a systematic review and meta-analysis. *Oncol. Nurs. Forum*. [Internet] 2014 Nov [Cited October 25, 2023]. 41(6):E326-E342. doi: 10.1188/14.ONF.E326-E342

[73] Brown, J. C., Huedo-Medina, T. B., Pescatello, L. S., Ryan, S. M., Pescatello, S. M., Moker, E., et al., (2012). The efficacy of exercise in reducing depressive symptoms among cancer survivors: a meta-analysis. *PLoS One*. [Internet]. 2012 Jan [Cited October 19, 2023]. 7(1), e30955. doi:10.1371/journal.pone.0030955

[74] Speck RM, Courneya KS, Masse LC, Duval S, Schmitz KH. An update of controlled physical activity trials in cancer survivors: a systematic review and meta-analysis. *J Cancer Surviv*. [Internet]. 2010Jun. [Cited October 19, 2023]. 4(2):87–100. doi:10.1007/s11764-009-0110-5

[75] American cancer society. Risks of cancer surgery. (n 55)

[76] Mayo Clinic. Chemotherapy. March 20, 2022; Accessed November 4, 2023]. Available from: https://www.mayoclinic.org/tests-procedures/chemotherapy/about/pac-20385033

[77] National Cancer Institute. Radiation therapy side effects. (n 41)

[78] Cancer Research Institute. Immunotherapy side effects. [online]. [November 2019; Accessed October 19, 2023]. Available from: https://www.cancerresearch.org/immunotherapy-side-effects

79 American Cancer Society. Targeted therapy side effects. [online]. [Accessed October 20, 2023]. Available from: https://www.cancer.org/cancer/managing-cancer/treatment-types/targeted-therapy/side-effects.html

[80] Centers for Disease Control and Prevention. Physical Activity. [online]. [August 1, 2023; Accessed October 20, 2023]. Available from: https://www.cdc.gov/physicalactivity/basics/pa-health/index.htm#:~:text=Regular%20physical%20activity%20is%20one,ability%20to%20do%20everyday%20activities.

[81] US Department of Health and Human Services. Physical activity guidelines for Americans. 2nd edition. [online]. [Accessed November 11, 2023]. 2018 Available from: https://health.gov/sites/default/files/2019-09/Physical_Activity_Guidelines_2nd_edition.pdf#page=39

[82] Centers for Disease Control and Prevention. Benefits of physical activity. [August 1, 2023; Accessed October 20, 2023]. Available from: https://www.cdc.gov/physicalactivity/basics/pa-health/index.htm#:~:text=Regular%20physical%20activity%20is%20one,ability%20to%20do%20everyday%20activities.

[83] National Heart, Lung, and Blood Institute. What is metabolic syndrome? [online]. [May 18, 2022; Accessed October 21, 2023]. Available from: https://www.nhlbi.nih.gov/health/metabolic-syndrome#:~:text=Metabolic%20syndrome%20

is%20a%20group,also%20called%20insulin%20resistance%20 syndrome.

[84] Centers for Disease Control and Prevention. Benefits of physical activity. (n 82)

[85] Centers for Disease Control and Prevention. Benefits of physical activity. (n 82)

[86] da Silveira MP, da Silva Fagundes KK, Bizuti MR, Starck É, Rossi RC, de Resende e Silva DT. Physical exercise as a tool to help the immune system against COVID-19: an integrative review of the current literature. *Clin Exp Med.* [Internet]. 2021 Feb. [Cited October 21, 2023]. 21(1):15-28. doi:10.1007/s10238-020-00650-3

[87] Cleveland Clinic. Natural killer cells. [online]. [October 4, 2023; Accessed October 21, 2023]. Available from: https://my.clevelandclinic.org/health/body/24898-natural-killer-cells#:~:text=NK%20cells)%3F-,Natural%20killer%20cells%20(NK%20cells)%20are%20white%20blood%20cells%20that,fighters%20in%20your%20immune%20system.

[88] Carter D. T cells, B cells and the immune system. [online]. [November 10, 2021; Accessed October 21, 2023]. Available from: https://www.mdanderson.org/cancerwise/t-cells--b-cells-and-the-immune-system.h00-159465579.html#:~:text=B%20cells%20create%20antibodies.&text=These%20antibodies%20bind%20to%20pathogens,help%20destroy%20an%20infected%20cell.

[89] BYJU'. Difference between monocytes and lymphocytes. [online]. Available from: https://byjus.com/biology/difference-between-monocytes-and-lymphocytes/#:~:text=Monocytes%20are%20the%20tools%20for,are%20tools%20for%20

Adaptive%2mmunity.&text=This%20was%20a%20brief%20introduction%20to%20the%20difference%20between%20monocyte%20and%20lymphocytes.

[90] Centers for Disease Control and Prevention. Benefits of physical activity. (n 82)

[91] American Society of Hematology. Blood basics. [online]. [Accessed October 22, 2023]. Available from: https://www.hematology.org/education/patients/blood-basics

[92] Harvard T.H. Chan. Fiber. [online]. [April 2022; Accessed October 22, 2023]. Available from: https://www.hsph.harvard.edu/nutritionsource/carbohydrates/fiber/

[93] Harvard T.H. Chan. Whole grains. [online]. [Accessed October 22, 2023]. Available from https://www.hsph.harvard.edu/nutritionsource/what-should-you-eat/whole-grains/

[94] Harvard T.H. Chan. Fiber. (n 92)

[95] Mayo Clinic Staff. Dietary fiber: Essential for a healthy diet. [online]. [Accessed October 22, 2023]. Available from: https://www.mayoclinic.org/healthy-lifestyle/nutrition-and-healthy-eating/in-depth/fiber/art-20043983#:~:-text=Soluble%20fiber%20is%20found%20in,with%20constipation%20or%20irregular%20stools.

[96] Harvard T.H. Chan. Fiber. (n 92)

[97] Mayo Clinic Staff. Dietary fiber: Essential for a healthy diet. (n 95)

[98] Watts M. Insoluble fibre and diabetes. [online]. January 15, 2019; [Accessed October 22, 2023]. Available from: https://www.diabetes.co.uk/nutrition/insoluble-fibre.html

[99] Harvard T.H. Chan. Whole grains (n 93)

[100] ASN Staff. Most Americans are not getting enough fiber in our diets. [June 9, 2021; Accessed October 22, 2023]. Available from: https://nutrition.org/most-americans-are-not-getting-enough-fiber-in-our-diets/

[101] Harvard T.H. Chan. Whole grains (n 93)

[102] American Heart Association. Dietary fats. [online]. [November 1, 2021; Accessed October 21, 2023]. Available from: https://www.heart.org/en/healthy-living/healthy-eating/eat-smart/fats/dietary-fats#:~:text=Dietary%20fats%20are%20essential%20to,and%20produce%20important%20hormones%2C%20too.

[103] Cleveland Clinic. Amino acids. [online]. [December 22, 2021; Accessed October 22, 2023]. Available from: https://my.clevelandclinic.org/health/articles/22243-amino-acids

[104] Ibid Cleveland Clinic. Amino acids.

[105] Piedmont. What is a complete protein? [online]. [Accessed October 21, 2023]. Available from: https://www.piedmont.org/living-better/what-is-a-complete-protein#:~:text=Which%20foods%20are%20complete%20proteins,Quinoa

[106] American Cancer Society. Constipation. [online]. [December 21, 2020; Accessed October 21, 2023]. Available from: https://www.cancer.org/cancer/managing-cancer/side-effects/stool-or-urine-changes/constipation.html

[107] American Cancer Society. Diarrhea. [online]. [February 1, 2020; October 21, 2023]. Available from: https://www.cancer.org/cancer/managing-cancer/side-effects/stool-or-urine-changes/diarrhea.html

[108] American Cancer Society. Chemo brain. [online]. [February 1, 2020; October 21, 2023]. Available from: Available from: https://www.cancer.org/cancer/managing-cancer/side-effects/changes-in-mood-or-thinking/chemo-brain.html

[109] America Cancer Society. Mouth sores and pain. [online]. [September 24, 2021; Accessed October 21, 2023]. Available from: https://www.cancer.org/cancer/managing-cancer/side-effects/eating-problems/mouth-sores.html

[110] Geffen JR, Herbst RS. Life-saving cancer cocktails. [online]. [June 2, 2008; Accessed October 23, 2023]. Available from: https://www.bottomlineinc.com/health/cancer-treatment/lifesaving-cancer-cocktails

[111] Marsden E, Nigh G, Birdsall S, Wright H, Traub M. Oncology Association of Naturopathic Physicians: Principles of Care Guidelines. *Curr. Oncol.* [Internet]. 2019 Feb 1 [Cited October 21, 2023]. 26(1):12-8. doi:10.3747/co.26.4815

[112] Ibid Marsden E, Nigh G, Birdsall S, Wright H, Traub M. Oncology Association of Naturopathic Physicians: Principles of Care Guidelines.

[113] Geffen JR, Herbst RS. Life-saving cancer cocktails (n 110)

[114] Marsden E, Nigh G, Birdsall S, Wright H, Traub M. (n 111)

[115] Smith JE, Richardson J, Hoffman C, Pilkington K. Mindfulness-Based Stress Reduction as supportive therapy in cancer care: systematic review. *J. Adv. Nurs.* [Internet] 2005 Nov. [Cited December 2, 2023]. 52(3):315-27. doi:10.1111/j.1365-2648.2005.03592.x

[116] Wang Y, Liu B, Han H, Hu Y, Zhu L, Rimm EB, et al. Associations between plant-based dietary patterns and risks of

type 2 diabetes, cardiovascular disease, cancer, and mortality – a systematic review and meta-analysis. *Nutr J.* [Internet]. 2023 Oct 4. [Cited October 23, 2023]. 22(1). doi.org/10.1186/s12937-023-00877-2

[117] Zhou X, Afzal S, Wohlmuth H, Münch G, Leach D, Low M, et al. Synergistic anti-inflammatory activity of ginger and turmeric extracts in inhibiting lipopolysaccharide and interferon-γ-induced proinflammatory mediators. molecules. [Internet]. 2022 Jun 16. [Cited November 25, 2023]. 27(12):3877. doi:10.3390/molecules27123877

[118] National Cancer Institute. Complementary and alternative medicine (CAM) for patients. [online]. [Accessed November 25, 2023]. Available from: https://www.cancer.gov/about-cancer/treatment/cam/patient

[119] National Cancer Institute. How do clinical trials work? [online]. [August 31, 2023; Accessed November 25, 2023]. Available from: https://www.cancer.gov/research/participate/clinical-trials/how-trials-work

[120] National Cancer Institute. Why participate in clinical trial? [online]. [September 18, 2023; Accessed November 25, 2023]. Available from: https://www.cancer.gov/research/participate/clinical-trials/why-participate

[121] American Cancer Society. Being in a clinical trial [August 18, 2020; Accessed November 25, 2023]. Available from: https://www.cancer.org/cancer/managing-cancer/making-treatment-decisions/clinical-trials/what-you-need-to-know/what-does-a-clinical-trial-involve.html

[122] American Cancer Society. Types and phases of clinical trials. [August 18, 2020; Accessed November 25, 2023].

Available from: https://www.cancer.org/cancer/managing-cancer/making-treatment-decisions/clinical-trials/what-you-need-to-know/phases-of-clinical-trials.html

[123] University of Virginia. Rights of a research participant. [online]. [Accessed November 25, 2023]. Available from: https://med.virginia.edu/clinicalresearch/participate-in-a-trial/rights-of-a-research-participant/#:~:text=To%20understand%20what%20part%20of,information%20will%20be%20kept%20private.

[124] US Department of Labour. Family and medical leave act. [online]. [Accessed November 27, 2023]. Available from: https://www.dol.gov/agencies/whd/fmla

[125] NHS Inform. Work and cancer. [online]. [April 12, 2023; November 27, 2023]. Available from: https://www.nhsinform.scot/illnesses-and-conditions/cancer/practical-issues/work-and-cancer/#:~:text=Under%20equality%20laws%2C%20your%20employer,usually%20get%20Statutory%20Sick%20Pay.

[126] Macmillan Cancer Support. Cancer and employment rights. [online]. [April 30, 2019; Accessed November 27, 2023]. Available from: https://www.macmillan.org.uk/cancer-information-and-support/impacts-of-cancer/work-and-cancer/cancer-and-employment-rights#:~:text=Cancer%20and%20the%20law,-If%20you%20have&text=There%20are%20laws%20that%20protect,Discrimination%20Act%201995%20protects%20you.

[127] Silver JK, Baima J, Mayer RS. Impairment-driven cancer rehabilitation: An essential component of quality care and survivorship. *CA A Cancer J Clinicians*. [Internet]. 2013

Sep. [Cited December 1, 2023]. 63(5):295-317. doi:10.3322/caac.21186

[128] Fann J. R., Thomas-Rich A. M., Katon W. J., Cowley D., Pepping M., McGregor B, Gralow J. Major depression after breast cancer: A review of epidemiology and treatment. *General Hospital Psychiatry*. [Internet]. 2008 Mar. [Cited December 1, 2023]. 30:112-126. doi:10.1016/j.genhosppsych.2007.10.008

[129] Kane D, Rajacich D, Andary C. Experiences of cancer patients' return to work. *CONJ*. [Internet]. 2020 Apr 17. [Cited December 1, 2023]. 30(2):113-8. doi:10.5737/23688076302113118

[130] Lebel S, Tomei C, Feldstain A, Beattie S, McCallum M. Does fear of cancer recurrence predict cancer survivors' health care use? *Support Care Cancer*. [Internet]. 2013 Mar. [Cited December 1, 2023]. 21(3):901-6. doi:10.1007/s00520-012-1685-3

[131] Herschbach P, Berg P, Dankert A, Duran G, Engst-Hastreiter U, Waadt S, et al. Fear of progression in chronic diseases. *J. Psychosom. Res.* [Internet] 2005 Jun. [Cited December 1, 2023]. 58(6):505-11. doi:10.1016/j.jpsychores.2005.02.007

[132] Gelse N, Bodschwinna D, Jarczok MN, Wanner M, Volz M, Mayer-Steinacker R, et al. Enhancing coping skills through brief interventions during cancer therapy – a quasi-experimental clinical pilot study. *Front Psychol*. [Internet]. 2023 Sep. [Cited December 1, 2023]. 7; 14. doi:10.3389/fpsyg.2023.1253423

[133] American Cancer Society. Cancer glossary: definitions & phonetic pronunciations. [online]. [December 2, 2023].

Available from: https://www.cancer.org/cancer/understanding-cancer/glossary.html

[134] Mayo Clinic. Search diseases & conditions. [online]. [Accessed December 2, 2023]. Available from: https://www.mayoclinic.org./

Disclaimer:

This book is designed as an educational and informational resource. It should not be used as a substitute for medical advice, diagnosis, or treatment recommendations. For personalised medical guidance and advice on potential treatments, it's important to consult with a qualified doctor who can address your specific medical condition.

About the Author

Romeo Richards, founder of 'The Healthcare Reform Campaign', established the organisation with a focus on enhancing patient care and improving conditions for healthcare professionals. His own health struggles highlighted the lack of easily understandable information about medical conditions for patients. Confronted with the need to make decisions about a newly diagnosed illness, Romeo was inspired to ensure accessible, patient-friendly information. His experience became the catalyst for advocating patient friendly resources for patients dealing with serious medical diagnosis. For further details about 'The Healthcare Reform Campaign' and its initiatives, please visit: https://www.romeorichards.com/healthcare-reforms/

Made in the USA
Las Vegas, NV
03 March 2024